Your Will Be Done

ANDREW MURRAY

Marshall Pickering

Pickering & Inglis Ltd
Marshall Pickering
34–42 Cleveland Street, London, W1P 5FB, U.K.

Copyright © 1989 Marshall Morgan & Scott Ltd
First published in book form in 1989
by Pickering & Inglis Ltd
Part of the Marshall Pickering Holdings Group

Clarion Classics are published by the Zondervan Publishing
House 1415 Lake Drive, S.E., Grand Rapids, Michigan 49506
North American Edition Copyright 1989 by the Zondervan
Corporation Grand Rapids, Michigan

British Library CIP Data

Murray, Andrew, *1828–1917*
   Your will be done
   1. Lord's Prayer – Critical studies
   I. Title   II. Series
   226.'9606

   ISBN 0–551–01863–1 (Marshalls)
         0–310–56102–7 (Zondervan)

Text set in 10/11pt Times Roman by Watermark, Hampermill
Cottage, Watford. Printed by Richard Clay Ltd, Bungay,
Suffolk.

CONTENTS

1 The Will of God, the Glory of Heaven   1

2 Doing God's Will: the Way to Heaven   6

3 Doing God's Will the Bond of Union with our Lord Jesus   10

4 The Will of God, the Salvation of the Perishing   15

5 The Heavenly Manna   19

6 Not Mine Own Will   23

7 Doing and Knowing God's Will   27

8 Even unto the Death   32

9 Lord! What Wilt Thou?   36

10 The Man after God's Own Heart   40

11 The Will of the Lord be Done   45

12 Of Knowing God's Will   49

13 God Working out His Own Will   53

14 Understanding the Will of God   58

15 Doing the Will of God from the Heart   62

16 Knowing and Not Doing   66

17 The Renewed Mind Proving God's Will   70

18 According to the Will of God   74

19 Filled with the Knowledge of God's Will   79
20 Standing Perfect in All the Will of God   83
21 The Will of God Your Sanctification   87
22 Unceasing Thanksgiving, the Will of God   92
23 The Salvation of All the Will of God   96
24 Lo, I Come to Do Thy Will   100
25 Doing the Will of God Obtains the Promise   105
26 God Himself Working His Will in Us   109
27 Suffering According to the Will of God   114
28 Living to the Will of God   119
29 Doing God's Will the Secret of Abiding   123
30 Prayer According to God's Will   127
31 The Glory of God's Will   131

Well Pleasing

 1 The Secret of Boldness Towards God   137
 2 God Himself Works It in You   140
 3 The Mark of God's Child   143
 4 Its Secret   146
 5 This Is the Lord's Doing   149
 6 The Lord Taketh Pleasure in His People   152

Chapter 1

The Will of God,
the Glory of Heaven

'Thy will be done in earth, as in heaven.'
Matthew 6:10

The will of a man is the power by which he determines his actions, and decides what he is to do or not to do. In it is manifested his hidden, inward being, proving what his desires and dispositions are, foolish or wise, good or evil. The will is the revelation of character and life. What a man truly wills, he will infallibly seek to have done, either by himself or through others.

In the will of God we have the perfect expression of his divine perfection. Because he is a fountain of all beauty and blessedness, his will is inconceivably beautiful and blessed. In it his divine wisdom and goodness make themselves known. Through it alone the creature can know his God; in accepting and doing that will he finds the only and the sure way to fellowship and union with God.

The glory and the blessedness of heaven consist in nothing but this, that God's will is done there in and by all. There is nothing to hinder God's working freely and fully all his blessed will in its countless hosts. To all that he wills for them of goodness and blessedness and service their whole being is surrendered in submission and adoration. God lives in them and they in God. They are filled with the fullness of God.

In the Lord's Prayer our Master teaches us to come to the Father with the wonderful petition, that his will may be done on earth, even as in heaven! He calls us to open our hearts to this and lift them heavenwards in real desire and prayer. He bids us count upon an answer, and according to the power that worketh in us, expect the experience in such measure as we are fitted for: God's will done in us and by us, on earth, as it is in heaven. The God who works it in heaven – is our Father who delights to work it on earth. The blessedness of earth cannot possibly be other than that of heaven: that our hearts desire and delight to have the will of God done.

Thy will be done, as in heaven, so on earth! Here is an invitation for you to come and meditate on this petition, if the Father will, by his Holy Spirit, show you the divine beauty of his will, and the altogether heavenly blessedness of living in it. Let us begin in this chapter by considering what God's will includes, that we may know aright what our Lord means and what we are to expect, when we pray: Thy will be done!

There is, first, the will of God's holy providence. Everything that happens on earth comes to the child of God as the will of his Father. In his infinite wisdom God so overrules all the evil of men and devils, that in permitting it, he can take it up into his will, and make it work out his purposes. Joseph says of the sin of his brethren: 'Ye thought evil against me, but God meant it unto good.' Jesus said to Pilate: 'Thou couldest have no power against me, except it were given thee from above.' In everything that came on him he saw God's will: it was all the cup the Father gave him. It is when the Christian learns to see God's will in everything that comes to him, grievous or pleasing, great or small, that the prayer, thy will be done, will become the unceasing expression of adoring submission and praise. The whole world, with its dark mysteries, and life, with all its difficulties, will be illumined with the light of God's presence and rule. And the soul will taste the rest and the bliss of knowing that it is every moment encircled and watched over by God's will, that nothing can separate it from the love of which the will is the expression. Happy the Christian who receives everything in Providence as the will of his Father.

There is, next, the will of God's righteous precepts. Every command of our Father in heaven is a ray of the divine will. Radiant to the eye that can see it, with all the perfection of the divine nature. It comes as a proof of the divine condescension, tenderly accommodating itself to our feebleness, as it puts the divine will into human words, suited to our special capacity and circumstances. We all naturally connect the rays of light on earth with the sun from which they come. The more the Christian learns to link every precept with the infinite will of love whence it comes, the more will he see the nobility and the joy of a life of entire obedience, the privilege and the honour of carrying out in human form the perfect will of the Father in heaven. He then learns to say of God's precepts what first appeared too high: They are the rejoicing of my heart. And, thy will be done, as in heaven, becomes the secret inspiration of a glad fulfilment of all God's commands.

Then comes – the will of God's precious promises. We often fail in the power of grasping or holding some promise, of which we fain would have the comfort, because we deal with it as a fragment, and do not connect it with the great whole of God's blessed will for us. Let every believer seek earnestly to realise what God's will in his promises is. It is his determination to do a certain thing.

His engagement to do it for or in me, if I will trust him. Behind the promise there is the faithful almighty God waiting to fulfil it. What a strength it would give in prayer, what a confidence in expectation, to be quiet, and trace the promise to the living will, the loving heart, that wills to make it true to every one that yields himself in trust and dependence. As, thy will be done, in view of God's providence, was the language of a glad submission, in view of his precepts, the surrender to a full obedience, so here, in relation to the promises, it becomes the song of an assured hope. Thy will be done, by thyself in us, O our Father in heaven.

One thought more – there is the will of God's eternal purpose. Our view of God's will in his providence, his precepts, his promises, is often very much confined to ourselves. The believer, who through these longs to enter fully into all the will of God, will be led on into a wider and a deeper insight into the glory of its counsels. He will learn something of that great purpose which filled the heart of God from eternity, which reveals nothing less than the triumph of God's redeeming love in a world of sin. As he is led by the Holy Spirit into the great counsels of redemption, into the meaning of the sacrifice by which God has sought to accomplish them, of the patience with which he is working out his plans, and the final triumph which is so sure and so glorious, he feels how little he has realised his position, or the meaning of this prayer. Thy will be done, as in heaven, so on earth, becomes the expression of his fellowship with God in his wondrous carrying out of his everlasting counsel of grace, of his intercession on behalf of a perishing world, of his joyful anticipation of all flesh seeing the glory of God. He feels himself as a unit floating in the sunlight of God's presence. He knows himself an instrument, a vessel, a member of the body of Christ, through which God's glory is working out his perfect will.

Believer, come and listen. This prayer needs your whole heart. It needs the teaching, yes, the indwelling of Jesus Christ in the heart, to be able to pray it aright. It calls for a heart, a will, a life entirely given up to the Father in heaven, by his Spirit dwelling in us, to understand it aright. Let the glory of God doing his will in us and through us be met by nothing less than a will wholly given up to his.

Chapter 2

Doing God's Will: the Way to Heaven

'Not everyone that saith unto me, Lord, Lord, shall enter into the kingdom of heaven; but he that doeth the will of my Father which is in heaven.' Matthew 7:21

We have seen that the will of God constitutes the glory of heaven. Heaven is nothing but the unhindered manifestation of the working of God's will, the shining out of his hidden glory in what he does. The inhabitants of heaven owe all their glory to God's working his will of love in them, and all their happiness to their working it out in his service. The petition in the Lord's Prayer teaches us to long and ask that earth may become like heaven, and that his will be done here as it is there. From this truth that of our text follows naturally. The only way to be fit to enter heaven must be to do the will of God here on earth. Every thought of heaven that does not lead us to do the will of God is a vain imagination.

There are multitudes of Christians who have never seen this. They think that the way to heaven is found in pious desires and religious duties, in trusting Christ for mercy, and seeking to be kept from gross sin. But the thought that Christ puts here – only those who love to do the will of God can enter heaven – has never taken possession of their mind or heart. And yet our Lord makes the difference between the religion of prayer and profession, and the religion of obedience and performance, as plain as words can make it. Not everyone that saith unto me Lord, Lord – that professes to acknowledge and honour me as Saviour – but he that doeth the will of my Father in heaven – he alone – shall enter the kingdom of heaven. It is the Father's presence and the Father's will in heaven that makes heaven what it is: doing the Father's will on earth is the only conceivable way of entering heaven: nothing can give the capacity for enjoying it. There must always be harmony between a life and its environment. To enter the heaven of God's will, without a nature that loves and does God's will, is an impossibility.

But from where, then, comes the terrible mistake that so many make, who think that they are honestly longing and striving to get to heaven? Let us try and answer this question. In everything that exists there is an outward form or shape, in which it manifests itself, and an inward power of life which constitutes its true nature or being. It is thus with heaven and our thought of it. Men regard it as a place full of brightness and glory and happiness – free from all sorrow or pain, full of all that can give rest and joy. And who would not wish to enter there? The most worldly hope to find a place in it when compelled to leave the present life. But they never think what attracts them is only an external image they form of heaven. And they know not that what constitutes the actual, essential glory of heaven, what really gives heaven and its inhabitants their rest and joy and everlasting song, is – the

presence of the Father who is in heaven, and the undis-
turbed supremacy of his holy will. Because in heaven
God's will does everything, and is done by everyone,
God's own blessedness fills all. Oh, the folly of thinking
of entering heaven while they are utterly incapable of
enjoying heaven. The Father in heaven, and his will on
earth as in heaven, are not the desire or joy of their
earth.

The same error, in mistaking the outward for the
inward, is made in regard to religion. God's Word calls
us to seek and to strive, listen to God's truth, to pray and
believe, to forsake sin and follow after that which is
good. And so men seek to put their trust in Christ, to
confess him, and do many things in his name, and think
that this is religion. And all the while they forget that the
inner spiritual reality of true religion is this – the knowing, and loving, and doing of the Father's will as their
one desire and delight. They know not that it is to work
this that Jesus is a Saviour from sin; that this is the only
proof that our faith is true; that by this path alone can the
entrance to heaven be found.

When this is preached, many a one comforts himself
with the thought of God's mercy. Did not Christ just
come for those who had sinned, and had not done God's
will? He did indeed, blessed be God! But not for those
who continue in sin, and do not make the will of God the
object of their life. Our sin and misery was that we had
fallen out of the will of God into our own will and the will
of Satan. Christ came with the one object of redeeming
us from the power of our own will, and giving us a new
nature and his Holy Spirit, to enable us here on earth to
love and do God's will. Without this, our Lord assures
us, there can be no thought of our entering heaven. The
same righteous grace that in justification receives the
ungodly into favour without works, through faith alone,
for the sake of Christ and his work, will in the great day
take the works and the life into account as the proof of
the reality of faith and union to Christ, and of the fitness
for entering heaven. As we are saved without works, we

are created in Christ Jesus for good works, which God had already prepared that we should walk in them. Without these there can be no entrance into heaven; they are indispensable. The Master's words are plain and decisive: He that doeth the will of my Father in heaven, shall enter into the kingdom of heaven.   Christ came from heaven to show us that doing the will of the Father is the one mark of a son of God, and so save us into doing that will true conversion is turning away from our self-will and giving ourselves to the will of God as our duty and our only blessedness. I ask every believer who reads this to enquire, and say whether he thinks that the doing of the Father's will, as the one object of Christ's salvation, and the one preparation for entering heaven, has taken the place in his life and faith and conduct, that it had in the life and teaching and conduct of Jesus Christ. Read the question over again, and pause; it is worth while giving a careful answer.

All salvation on earth or in heaven is – doing the will of God. If we find that this blessed truth has never shone with its full heavenly light into our souls, let us at once turn to our Lord Jesus and ask him to teach us. Let us give ourselves up to it, to study, to believe, to practise, to rejoice in it. Let us each day choose the will of God, his whole will, and nothing but his will, to have rule over us and dwell within us. The living Father, whose love can make it our blessedness, through the living Christ, who loves to teach it to us and work it in us, will enable us to do his will.

Chapter 3

Doing God's Will the Bond of Union with our Lord Jesus

'Whosoever shall do the will of my Father which is in heaven, the same is my brother, and sister, and mother.'
Matthew 12:50

How many Christians there are who long greatly for a more intimate fellowship with the Lord Jesus. The thought of a fuller experience of his love, of his abiding presence, of his mighty power to save from sin and self greatly attracts them. They often wonder that the longings and the prayers of years appear to avail so little. They are ready to turn to any one who they think can help them to discover the secret of what they have sought in vain, the full manifestation in their heart of the love and the power of Christ. Come, my reader, turn today to our blessed Lord himself, and let him tell you his open secret. The way into the most intimate union with Christ is very simple: doing the will of his Father. Of one who does this he says: the same is my brother and sister and mother.

What does this mean? A brother or a sister, or one who is born of the same father, shares the same love, and home, and care; bears in some measure the same likeness in disposition and character; is bound to his other brothers and sisters by these ties in a common love. When Christ calls one of us a brother or sister, it means nothing less. Like him, we are born of God: the Father's life, and love, and likeness are in us, as in him. As the elder brother, he gives to us and shares with us all he has; he pours out on us all the love with which the Father loves him. He is not ashamed to call us brethren. He delights in our relationship to him, in our welfare, in our society. He only lives to find his happiness in us, and in what he can do for us. The one thing he longs for is that we should know and claim our relationship, should come to him and be free with him as no brother or sister ever was.

Let us pray for the quickening of the Holy Spirit to make all this a reality. Just think of what a joy would come into the believer's life if he truly realised this: Jesus loves me as a brother, yes me, just as I am, all unworthy and sinful. He loves me as a brother. No elder brother ever watched over a weak younger brother so tenderly, as my elder brother watches over me. He wants me to know it. He gives the command: 'Say to my brethren, I ascend to my Father and your Father.' He wants me to know it; he longs that I should live with him as a brother in the Father's presence: he is able and willing to make the possibility a reality. He invites us to come and say in tender reverence, O my holy elder brother – I dare scarce say, and yet I may and I will – I am thy brother; thou art my brother. He can enable us to realise it and abide in his presence all the day and every day.

And what is the disposition of heart that can claim the blessing and abide in it? Read again: 'Whosoever shall do the will of my Father which is in heaven, the same is my brother and sister and mother.' The Lord opens here to us the deepest secret of his own life as Son of God on earth. He came as man to prove the blessedness and the glory of doing the will of the Father. In his human life this was the one disposition that lay at the root of his power to conquer sin, to satisfy God, and to save us. Doing the will of God is the only possible way, on earth or in heaven, of pleasing him. Thinking as God thinks, loving what God loves, willing as God wills, doing what God says – how could we think that there is any way but this to the fellowship or the favour of God? Of himself Jesus said: 'I have kept the commandments of my Father and abide in his love.' The law for the elder brother is the unchangeable law for all the children: doing the Father's will is the only true mark of being a child. And so it is the one condition of being admitted to the full experience of a walk in all the joy that the brotherhood of Jesus can bring. Doing the will of the Father is the bond of union with Jesus. The converse is also true. Union with Jesus gives the power to do the will of the Father. We begin with 'willing to do his will', and so it is as far as we know and can. When this is really done with the whole heart, we come and claim the promise of being admitted consciously into the love and society of the elder brother. In true communion with him, studying his example, drinking in his spirit, receiving his strength, we get larger insight and greater love of God's will, and begin to long to live in it wholly even as Jesus did. In ever closer union with him, the elder brother imparts to us, in even deeper measure, the secret of his own blessed life in the will of God.

And what is the secret? It is found in the words our

Lord so frequently uses – 'the will of my Father, which is in heaven.' Christ was only able to do and suffer as he did, because it was all to him each moment the will of a loving Father. The will of the Father was nothing but the experience of the love of the Father: therefore he delighted, therefore he was able, to do it. Many Christians never learn to understand the difference between the law of God and the will of God. The law is given by a ruler, and when embodied in a statute book, may be kept or broken, with very little thought of personal relationship to the law-giver. For this reason the law has no power to secure obedience. Christ speaks of the will as the will of the Father: the expression of a personal living communication, in which the Father's voice and presence is ever known, and the will never for a moment separated from him whose it is. It was the ever-present love of God showing his will, and the ever-blessed enjoyment of that love, that enabled Christ to be obedient even unto death. It is this alone that can enable us to do the Father's will. The grace once for all to yield ourselves to do only that will: the faith to believe that in the fellowship and by the power of Christ such a life is possible; the joyful devotion to him to walk as led by his hand, and like him to do the Father's will; these all come as a believer seeks to know the life of a brother of the first begotten Son.

It is indeed a change in the life of a believer when he fully grasps and experiences the difference between the law of God and the will of the Father. He sees how the only power to do the will is the unceasing experience of the Father's presence, his loving voice, his guiding eye, his inspiring love. He sees how that was the life Jesus lived, how nothing less is the life Christ lives in us. He learns to understand how doing the Father's will is the one blessing into which faith is to lead us, the one secret of abiding union with Christ Jesus. Go out, my soul, into thy work this day, and let thy life be transfigured by the one thought: like Jesus, with Jesus, in Jesus, I live to do the Father's will. And as you fail, or fear to fail, just whisper: O my Lord, my elder brother, thou and I, thou and I, are we not one in doing the Father's will.

Chapter 4

The Will of God, the Salvation of the Perishing

'Even so it is not the will of your Father which is in heaven, that one of these little ones should perish' Matthew 18:14

Our Lord Jesus here uses the words, 'little ones', both of the children of whom he spoke in verses 2 and 3, and also of the feeble and simple ones among his people: 'The little ones who believe in me' (Matt 18:6). He says that just as surely as a man rejoices over one lost sheep, that he has found again, so the Father does not will that any one, even of the feeblest and most despised, should perish. When our Lord spoke elsewhere of his doing the Father's will, it was specially the will of God to save the lost that he meant: 'I am come down from heaven, not to do mine own will, but the will of him that sent me. And this is the will of him that sent me, that of all that which he giveth me I should lose nothing. For this is the will of my Father, that every one that beholdeth the Son, and believeth on him, should have eternal life.' The will of the Father is the salvation of men. All the leadings of God's will, down to the minutest details of the life of every hour, have their root in this great fountain of redeeming love: that not one of the little ones should perish. Christ's coming from heaven, all his speaking and doing, his living and suffering and dying, it all had its unity in this – it was the revelation of God's will to save, and of Christ's surrender of himself to do that will in saving all the Father had given him.

When we yield ourselves to do the Father's will, must the will of God for the salvation of men be to us, as it was to Christ, the main object of our life, the one thing we do? It must indeed. The life that was in Christ is the same life that is in us. The glory of the Father; the blessedness of being the channels of the Father's love; the entire surrender to the one work the Father wants done in the world; all these claim our devotion as much as they did that of Christ. There is an infinite difference in the part he took and the part we are to take in carrying out that will: but the will itself is to be as much the joy and the aim of our life as it was of his. The larger our apprehension of God's will, and the more complete our surrender to it in all its breadth, to be wholly possessed of it, the more surely will we grow to the stature of the perfect man in Christ Jesus, and reach our Christian maturity.

It is just here that so many Christians fail. They seek to know the will of God only in its minute details concerning themselves, and so they live practically under a law consisting in commandments and ordinances. Their own personal happiness is the first thing; obedience and sanctification are subordinate to these, as means to an end; the selfish element infects and enfeebles all their religion. They have no conception of the nobility, of the heavenly royalty of spirit, that comes to the man who forgets and loses himself, as he gives himself away to that will of God for the salvation of men. It was that will that sent Christ into the world. It was that will that animated him during his whole life. It was for the breathing that will into our hearts and lives that the Holy Spirit came. It is in the being possessed by that will, even as Christ was possessed by it, yielding ourselves to the mastery of divine love, that the image of God is restored in us, so that we may live only to love and to bless even as God does.

'It is not the will of your Father which is in heaven that one of these little ones should perish.' What inspiration these words have given to God's workers on behalf of orphans, of waifs and strays, of children in India perishing from famine, or in Africa from slavery. What courage to thousands of teachers for the little ones of whom they had charge. What patience and strength it has breathed into the hearts of those who have had to deal with the neglected and the outcast in every land. It was their joy and hope that they knew that they were doing the will of God. Yes more, they knew that the mighty will of God was working itself out through them. These all have experienced how blessed it was at times to look away from their own little and limited interests and duties, and to cast themselves into the mighty stream of God's loving will which is slowly but surely working out his blessed purpose. There they found themselves in fellowship with God's own Son, and with the saints of all ages, whose one glory it had been that they had known and fulfilled the redeeming will of God.

What a change it would bring into the life of many a believer to know and love this will of the Father, to lose self and sacrifice all in order to be mastered and consumed by its blessed fire. If you would thus know it, reader, and be possessed by it, you must make it a definite object of study and desire. Seek in meditation to get some right impression of its glory. Ask for the Holy Spirit's teaching to give you a spiritual vision of the infinite energy of the divine love, as it wills nothing but good to every one of its creatures. It needs time and thought and prayer; it needs the giving up of all our self-satisfaction with our limited views of God's will. It needs above all, the indwelling of the Christ, in whom that will realised and manifested itself, to make us partakers of his own Spirit and disposition. We then can know something of that infinite will of love working itself out through us, filling the little vessel of our will out of its own living stream, and making the will of God indeed our will.

We have seen that it is doing the will of God that is the glory of heaven, the way to heaven, our likeness to the elder brother, and the food of our spiritual life. Let us begin doing the will of God in this aspect too, really giving ourselves to him for the saving of the lost. It will waken within us the capacity of apprehending better the glory of the divine will that none of the little ones should perish, and the divine privilege of our being made partakers of it. There is no other way for us to the fellowship of God but to have one will with him. And there is no way to this but through Christ and the participation of his Spirit. As we apprehend intelligently who and what the Christ is and his true life, the Son who has come to work out the Father's will and love, and accept none other but this Christ as our Lord and our life, the hope will arise that this redeeming will can master us too as its vessels and channels, that we too can go through the world filled with a divine life, the divine will inspiring and energising our will, and life passing out from us to those who are perishing.

Chapter 5

The Heavenly Manna

'I have meat to eat that ye know not of. My meat is to do the will of him that sent me, and to finish his work.' John 4:32,34

When tempted in the wilderness by Satan to satisfy his hunger by a miracle, Christ answered: Man shall not live by bread alone, but by every word that proceedeth out of the mouth of God. The life is more than bread. God's Word, received and obeyed, is the true nourishment of our life. In the Beatitudes Christ said: Blessed are they that hunger and thirst after righteousness, after the doing of what is right; they shall be satisfied. And so he says here of himself that to do the will of him that sent him, and to finish his work, is the meat that he eats, the food by which he lives. The hidden manna is God's will; to do it is to eat and live. Let us think what this eating teaches us.

Eating means the maintenance of life. All created life

must be supported by nourishment from without, if it is not to die. And the food must ever be in correspondence to the nature of the life it sustains, and the organs provided for receiving it. Our physical life is fed from the life of nature. Our spiritual life can only be maintained out of the eternal life that is in God. There is no way for our receiving that life, day by day, but by doing the will of God. The life of God reveals and communicates itself only in his will. In its first beginning life is always a gift. But its maintenance is always connected with action and growth. It is doing God's will, and accomplishing his work that will secure to the Christian the daily continuance in the divine life.

Eating means appropriation. Our body receives from the outer world of which it is a part, that by which it lives, the constituent elements by which its life is sustained. These can nourish us in no other way but by being taken up into our system, assimilated and made a very part of our own selves. This is how it is in the spiritual life. As we have said already, the life of God acts and manifests itself through the will of God. And it is only by truly and fully appropriating that will, taking it into our system, wholly assimilating it, and making it a part of our own being, by doing it, that the life can be maintained in us. The life is a hidden spiritual mystery; the will is its concrete expression, capable of being known, and accepted or rejected. And because the will is the divine power in action, so there is no possible way of assimilating the divine will, but by action on our part – that is, by our doing it. It is not the knowledge, or the admiration, or the approval of the will of God, but the doing of it, that alone feeds the heavenly life. It is only by doing that I really make it my own. 'My meat is to do his will.'

Eating means the renewal and increase of strength. We do not eat just enough to maintain a bare existence; we desire to have food, both in quantity and quality, sufficient to give us strength and vigour for our work. Doing God's will is the sure way to become strong. Many Christians seek their strength in prayer, in faith, in the promises, in fellowship. They complain of their feebleness. They have never learnt that Christ made doing the will of the Father his meat; it was this that was rewarded with the divine strength for all he had to do. He felt that he had but one thing to do in the world – to finish the work for which God had sent him; as he did it he received new strength for what he still had to do. It is this his disciples need. As I appropriate God's will, and know I am doing the very thing God is willing for me, its power works in me. Doing the will of God brings heavenly strength.

Eating means satisfaction. God has created a sense of need in us. Hunger impels us to seek food, and makes our partaking of it an enjoyment and a source of satisfaction. 'Bless the Lord … who satisfieth thy mouth with good things; so that thy youth is renewed like the eagle's.' 'He satisfieth the hungry soul.' It is feeding on the will of God that gives this divine satisfaction. The will of God is his glory and perfection; doing that will leads up into the wonderful fellowship and partnership with himself. But that does not mean, doing what is right, or doing what the law commands. No, the right things may be done under the constraint of conscience or duty, without bringing real satisfaction. It is only when what we do is doing as the will of the Father, in the sense of his presence, in fellowship with himself, and the loving desire to please him, that it will give nourishment and strength and satisfaction to the soul.

There are many Christians who mourn over their leanness and their feebleness. They study Christ's image and example, they seek in some things to be conformed to him, and yet find so little either of the power or the joy of living as he lived. The cause is simple. They do not feed on the food on which Christ fed. Two children, or two men, may be equally healthy, but the difference of food may make all the difference between their strength and success in the work of life. The believer has the same eternal life that was in Christ Jesus. But it needs the same daily food, if there is to be any measure of that conformity which God expects and has provided for. Our Lord tells us: My meat is that I do the will of him that sent me. He that eats of this meat shall have the life more abundant, shall be satisfied as with marrow and fatness.

And what can be the reason of so much failure in feeding on this heavenly food? It may be that the church has not taught it as clearly as was needed, or that we heard and heeded not, or that when we did heed, we were deceived by the lie of Satan that this was too hard a path. And yet the Lord has said it so plainly: The will of God is the glory of heaven; the doing of God's will ought to be our great prayer on earth. The doing of God's will is the only pass to heaven; the only mark of the family likeness in the home of Jesus. The doing of God's will is the only food on which a child of God can thrive and be able to finish the work the Father has given us to do. The doing of God's will is our daily food: we must go back upon our past life and see if this has been what we have been feeding on. And if not, we must believe that a change of diet, a return to the simple heavenly fare on which the Son of God lived his life and did his work, will restore us to health and make the work of God our joy and our life.

Soul, pray for a great hunger for the will of God, as natural and as continual as for your daily bread. Beg, even if it were at first but for a crumb of this heavenly bread from the Father's table, God showing you his will for you, and enabling you to do it for him. It may be the beginning of such a change in your life. The work you have done for God, at your choice and in your way, and the commandments you have tried to obey, may all become to you the loving will of the living Father. Instead of eating the bread you had to find for yourself you will say: 'I have meat to eat ye know not of' – the will of the Father made known and performed, day by day.

Chapter 6

Not Mine Own Will

'I can of mine own self do nothing: as I hear, I judge: and my judgment is just; because I seek not mine own will, but the will of the Father which hath sent me.' John 5:30

The will of God is the power by which the universe exists from moment to moment. It is by the unceasing active exercise of his will that the sun shines, and that every lily is clothed with beauty. There is no goodness, or strength, or beauty, but as he wills it. The glory and blessedness of heaven are nothing but the working of his will. The hosts of heaven live with their wills turned and opened to him, and find their happiness in allowing his will to do its perfect work in them. When the blessed Son became man to lead us in the way to God, he told us that the whole secret of his life was, not doing his own will, but yielding himself so to do the will of the Father, that his will should receive and work out that which the will of the Father worked in him. He said that he had been sent, and that he had delighted to come, for the one purpose, with his human will and his human body, to do not his own will, but the will of the Father. He set us the example of a man, a true man, finding his blessedness and his way to God's glory, in the absolute surrender to God's will. He thus showed us what the duty was for which man was created, and what the new life he was to bring his people. In such entire dependence on God, as to do nothing of himself, and to judge nothing but as he heard from the Father, he was able always to give a righteous judgment. He could count upon God to give him all the wisdom and the strength he needed, to work out his own will perfectly in him. All for the one simple reason: 'Because I seek not mine own will, but the will of him that sent me.'

'Not mine own will, but the will of him that sent me!' But had our Lord Jesus his own will, a will different from the Father's, that he needed to say: Not my will? Had he a will that needed to be denied? Undoubtedly. But was not such a will sin? By no means. This was the glory of the creation of man that he had a self-hood, his own will, a power of self-determination, by which he was to decide what he should be. This was not sin, that man had his own desire and thought and will. Without this he could not be a free creature. He had a will, with which to decide whether he should act according to the will of God or not. Sin only came when man held to his own will as creature in opposition to the will of God. As man, made like unto us in all things, 'in all points tempted like as we are, yet without sin,' Christ had a human will; for instance to eat when he was hungry, or to shrink from suffering, when he saw it coming. We know how in the temptation in the wilderness, he kept the former, in the prospect of his death, the latter, in perfect subjection to the Father's will. (Matt 4:4; Luke 12:50; John 12:27.) It is just this that gives its infinite worth to his sacrifice; it was the unceasing sacrifice of his human will to the Father. 'I seek not mine own will, but the will of him that sent me.'

These words reveal to us the inmost meaning of Christ's redemption. They teach us what the life is for which we were created, and out of which we fell in paradise. They show us wherein the sinfulness of that fallen state consists out of which Christ came to deliver us: he seeks to free us from our selfwill. They reveal to us the true creature life and the true Son – life, perfect oneness of will with God's will. They open too us the secret power of Christ's redeeming work – atoning for our self-will by his loyalty at all costs to God's will; and the true nature of the salvation and the life he gives us – the will and the power to say: I delight to do thy will, O God. Every spirit seeks a form in which to embody itself: these words give the highest revelation of the life in which the spirit that was in Christ embodied itself in him, and embodies itself in all who seek truly and fully to accept his salvation to the uttermost. I seek not my will, but the will of him that sent me, is the keynote of the only life well-pleasing to the Father on earth, and fit for his fellowship in heaven.

How little God's children know the Christ he has given them. And how little the true nature of the salvation Christ came to bring. How many there are who have never been taught that salvation out of self-will into doing God's will is alone true blessedness. And how many who, if they think they know it as a truth, never set themselves to seek this first as the true entrance into the kingdom of God and his righteousness. And yet this is in very deed what Christ revealed, and promised, what he secured on Calvary, and bestowed from heaven in the Holy Spirit. How can we become possessed of this blessed life?

I have pointed out previously how great the difference is between the idea of the law of a state, as contained in a statute book, and the will of a king to whom one stands in a personal relationship. If we would truly, however distantly, follow in Christ's footsteps, we must stand with him in the same close personal relationship to the

Father. Without this the most earnest efforts to do the Father's will must prove a failure. When our Lord so often spoke of 'The will of my Father, which is in heaven,' he wanted us to understand that it was the living personality and love that was at once motive and power for the obedience. When he spoke 'of the will of him that sent me,' he showed that it was not only the consciousness of having a work, but the desire of pleasing the one who sent him, that was the mainspring of all he did. We need the sense of the presence and nearness of the God whose will we are to do as much as our Lord did. Separate the thing you have to do from him whose will it is, and it becomes a burden and an impossibility. Live in the faith that he has sent you, that it is his living loving will, over which he watches, which he himself even works out, that you are doing – instead of its being a burden you are to carry, it becomes a power that carries you. The will of the Father is such a beautiful, wise, gentle, loving will, that to know it as the breathing out of the heart of God, makes it an infinite attraction and delight.

And how can we enter into this experience of the Father's nearness, and thus be able to do everything as his will? There is only one way. Jesus Christ must work it in us. And that not as from without, strengthening our faculties or assisting our efforts. No, this blessed doing of the Father's will is the mark of his life as Son. He can work it in us, as we yield ourselves wholly and receive him truly to dwell in us. It is right and needful that we should set ourselves with all earnestness and make the attempt. It is only by its failure that we really learn how entirely he must and will do all. So inseparably is this 'seeking not mine own will, but the will of him that sent me,' connected with Jesus Christ, that it is only when he comes in and manifests himself in the heart and dwells there, that he can work this full salvation in us. 'Blessed are they that hunger and thirst after righteousness, for they shall be filled.'

Chapter 7

Doing and Knowing God's Will

'If any man will do his will, he shall know of the doctrine, whether it be of God, or whether I speak of myself.' John 7:17

There was great division among the Jews as to who Christ really was, and the divine authority of the truth he taught. They wanted some sign as a clear proof that he was really come from God. Christ's answer tells them that the proof depended upon the state of their heart.

A man who wants the divine evidence of Christ's mission while he is not ready to do God's will, seeks for it in vain. A man whose will is set upon doing God's will, as far as he knows it, is alone in the fit state for receiving further divine illumination.

Our Lord says: 'If any man will do his will, he shall know of the doctrine, whether it be of God.' He speaks of two things: the will of God we are to do, and the teaching about God we are to know. He tells us the second is entirely dependent upon the first. As we will to do, we shall be able to know. It is the contrast and the connection of precept and promise. Will, that is, be ready, be determined to do God's will, and you shall have divine light and certainty as to all that Jesus has taught. The commands are simple and easy to be understood: he that seeks honestly to do them in the fear of God will learn to know the mystery of Christ. A will, a disposition, set upon doing God's will, is the only organ for knowing God's truth.

There are many Christians who complain of their lack of spiritual discernment. The promises of Christ, in this very gospel of St John, appear beyond their reach. They would fain know that 'the doctrine is of God'; they would like to experience and to feel that it is of divine origin, and in divine efficacy; that God himself confirms and makes the words true as a living power. Take the promise of Christ in this chapter, of streams of living water flowing out of the believer. Or, later on, of the life more abundantly; of his followers not walking in darkness, but having the light of life; of our doing greater works than he had done; of his manifesting himself to us; of his and the Father's dwelling in us; of our abiding in him and he in us; of our asking what we will, and having it given to us. When a man really knows the teaching is from God, has the truth and power of God in it, it becomes easy to believe it, and receives its fulfilment. To all believers who really long to have these promises shine with divine light in their hearts, Christ's message comes today: it all depends upon the one thing, that you really will to do the will of God. Let us try and take hold of the lessons we need.

Christ teaches us that in the growth of the Christian life faith depends upon character. Just as, at conversion, there can be no faith without repentance, so on through life, faith cannot grow or inherit the promises, without a life given up to the doing of God's will. 'Some having

thrust from them a good conscience, have made ship-
wreck of the faith.' The great reason why so many pray
for an increase of faith and never get it, is that 'the will
to do God's will' has never taken the place it must have.
The will rules the life; the will is the index of the heart;
the whole man is to be judged by the will; unless there be
a fixed resolve, a seeking with the whole will, to do the
will of God, there can be no growth in faith or the knowledge of the divine truth to which it gives access. It is only
as God's will is truly and fully taken up into my willing
and doing, that God can reveal himself to me.

God judges our conduct by the will. Our Lord says, 'If
any man will do his will.' A believer may in his youth,
through ignorance or feebleness, fail in doing the will; if
he who searches the heart sees that he indeed wills, longs
and thirsts to do it, God will see in this the heart that is
ready for spiritual light. 'If there first be a ready mind, it
is accepted according to that a man hath, and not according to that he hath not.' A believer, as in Romans chapter 7, may be able to say before God that he delights in
the law of God after the inward man, and yet have to
mourn his terrible failure. If there be this will really to
do, his failure will lead him on to see how Romans 7:2–4
is the deliverance from the law of sin in the members by
the law of the spirit of life in Christ Jesus, so that the
righteousness of the law is fulfilled in them that walk
after the spirit. Christ's words are not meant for those
who content themselves with the idea that they will to do
the will while they do not press on to the life in the spirit,
in which God works both to will and to do. It is the heart
where the will is indeed, with its whole strength, act
upon God's will, that the divine truth and power of
Christ's teaching will be known.

To do the will of God the first step is thus to take it up
into our will. The will of God is the heavenly treasure in
the earthen bowl of our will, that the excellency of the
power may be of God and not of us and we so learn to
trust God to work his own will in us and through us. I
cannot repeat the message too frequently or too earn-

estly: the one object for which our will was given us, its true nobility and blessedness, is that with it we might take in and make our own the very will that God has. Before I see all that that will implies, or feel that I have the power to perform it, let me regard it as the one thing God asks from me, the one thing I can do to please him and become a partaker of his blessedness – day by day to accept, to worship, to will his blessed will, and to do it. He works in us both to will and to do.

'Willing to do the will' of God is the sure way to all growth in spiritual knowledge and experience. Actually doing all that is within the reach of my spiritual stature, and willing with the whole heart to do all, is the single eye which ensures the whole body being full of divine light. The great reason why so much Bible study and prayer for divine guidance is so fruitless is this – the heart is not in the right state for receiving God's teaching. Peter writes 'Ye have purified your souls in obeying the truth': it is the actual doing of God's will, with the entire surrender to God to do it wholly and unceasingly, in the greatest things and in the least, that purifies the soul, and inherits the promise: 'Blessed are the pure in heart, for they shall see God.' There is in the will of God such a divine vitality and energy, that to the heart that wills and does it, not merely as a matter of duty or Christian training, but because God has willed it, and even as God wills it, it becomes life and strength. The spiritual knowledge of God, of his presence, his power, his indwelling is given to the obedient: 'If a man love me, he will keep my words: and my Father will love him, and we will come unto him, and make our abode with him.'

Here is the way to a strong and joyful spiritual life. Unite yourself to the will of God; it will unite you to him; it will draw him to you. Will with all your will, what God wills; make this the chief exercise of your spiritual life; as much as you truly have of God's will, you have of God. Our Lord said: 'I am the way, the truth, and the life.' He was this because he came not to do his own will, but the will of the Father. This is the one way in which he will lead you. The new and living way he opened up in his blood. This is the one truth he will be to you, that in the doing of the Father's will, is the union with him perfected. This is the one life he will given you, the life of God given in Christ, revealed and perfected by the will of God, as it is willed and done by us.

Chapter 8

Even unto the Death

*'Father, if thou be willing, remove this cup
from me: nevertheless not my will, but thine,
be done.'* Luke 22:42

Gethsemane! The inmost sanctuary of the life of our
Lord, and his great redemption. In some respects more
mysterious than even Calvary. Of the visible suffering
and sacrifice on the cross, the garden opens up the inner
meaning and power. And of all the suffering of
Gethsemane, 'Not my will, but thine, be done' was the
key. It shows us what it was that made the great sacrifice
a necessity, our self-will; what the disposition was that
gave it its worth, the surrender of the will to receive
God's will; what the redemption was that it effected, the
conquest and atonement of our self-will; and what the
salvation it actually brings, the impartation of a will
given up to God. Come, my soul, be still, and worship in
holy fear, as thou seest what it cost thy Lord to speak the

words thou so easily sayest. Learn from him what fullness of meaning and blessing there is to be found in them.

Now we look at the sin Christ dies for. Why is the Son of God here on his way to the death of the cross? What is it that costs him all this agony and suffering? It is sin that needs this sacrifice; it is to take away sin that he is here. And the first part of his work in taking it away is that he himself resists and conquers it. It is this death struggle with sin that cost him the agony. All through his life he had been 'in all points tempted like as we are, yet without sin.' In this last hour of the powers of darkness they make one great assault on the very citadel of his being, and seek to tempt him with the sorest of all temptations – following his own will as his nature shrank back from the awful curse-bearing that was set before him. The scene reveals to us what is the deepest root of all sin the assertion of our self-will. This was the sin and the fall of Adam. This is the source of all evil on earth. It is this, in the believer, the hidden cause of all failure and disappointment. God's will is the living power through which his love communicates itself and its blessings to the creature. Man's will was meant to be the power by which he was intelligently to yield himself and co-operate with God in receiving and appropriating all the divine nature had to impart. Self-will, a will not yielded to God, is, in the whole universe of things, the only thing that hinders God in revealing and communicating his blessedness to the creature. The cross is the proof of man's self-will in the refusal to bow to God's Son. Christ's agony in Gethsemane is the proof that it is this same sin that he came to conquer and cast out.

Now we turn to the victory Christ won. We often look upon the suffering of Christ with the endurance of the curse and death of the cross, as the cause of our salvation. Scripture teaches us to look to what gave that suffering and death its inner value: Christ's obedience. It was not merely in what he did or suffered, but in the spirit in which he acted, that its infinite worth, its atoning merit is to be found. During his whole life he had spoken of not doing his own will. Here he proves that he will do the will of the Father, even though it cost him his life. Even unto death, he says: Not my will! And so through death, in dying to his own will, he teaches us what God claims as his right, and what alone can bring us to our true place of blessing – the entire losing and giving up of our will and life to God's will as the way into the life and glory of God.

We move on to consider the atonement Christ accomplished. And now, the victory of Christ over man's self-will, how does it profit and save us? In two ways, as we regard him in his substitution or his fellowship, as the Christ for us, as the Christ in us. In the former of these aspects, his victory over sin as self-will, his obedience unto death and his infinite acceptableness in the Father's sight, becomes ours the moment we believe in him. As those who are united to him by faith, his righteousness and merit, with all the Father's delight in him on account of them, are made our very own: 'We are made the righteousness of God in him.' The sin of our self-will is blotted out. We are dealt with by God as if we never had sinned: counted righteous, and allowed to look up to God in his beloved Son as altogether well-pleasing to him. Were there but any due sense of the awfulness of the sin of self-will, especially in God's redeemed children, with what joy would the assurance of its being blotted out be welcomed. And how fervent would be the longing to know to the full the fruit of the victory Christ has achieved for us in freeing us from its power as well as its guilt.

Now we consider the salvation Christ bestows. This is the second aspect of Christ's victory: he has freed us from the dominion of self-will. The very nature and essence of the salvation he imparts is, what was the very nature and essence of his own life, a delight and power to do God's will alone. Gethsemane teaches us the way to receive the full experience of the deliverance. Just as there was in Christ, in his holy sinless nature, a learning of obedience through what he suffered, until it culminated in the surrender of his will unto the death, so there may be in the believer, who seeks to follow his Lord in full conformity, such a growth, both in insight into the absolute necessity of a giving up of all self-will, even in the least things, and also in the divine certainty of God's working in us, what Christ has won for us, that he is led to know experimentally what it is that he is crucified with Christ, and dead to self and its will. But there can be no thought of our understanding or attaining this, until the desire has come to give up all, even unto death, to live in the will of God alone.

Believer, is this the very Christ you delight in and seek to be conformed to, and long to know fully in his indwelling power? In Gethsemane he entered into the very deepest and nearest fellowship with you in surrendering his will to the death: enter you there into the deepest and nearest fellowship with him in surrendering your will as he did. Pray for the Holy Spirit to show you how self-will is the root of all sin and temptation and darkness; how the will of God can come in and cast it out and live in you; how faith in Christ who died to conquer our self-will, and now waits to dwell in us, can make you partake of his death and victory. Learn the lesson that death to self-will just means a quiet bowing before God in utter poverty and helplessness, and a simple trusting in the blessed lamb of God, who passed through death as the only way to the perfect surrender of his will to God's will, to breathe his own Spirit into us.

To a soul longing to live only and wholly in the will of God, death to all self-will is the one inevitable demand, but also in the faith of Christ Jesus the one sure and most blessed deliverance.

Chapter 9

Lord!
What Wilt Thou?

*'And Saul ... trembling and astonished said,
Lord, what wilt thou have me to do?* Acts 9:6

On the prayer, Thy will be done, as in heaven so in earth, there needs to follow the more special one, Lord! what wilt thou have me to do? Men have often asked what was the secret of the wonderful consecration and power which we see in the life of Paul. At his conversion, his first act, after he knew the Lord who had met him, was the surrender of his will. Lord! what wilt thou have me to do? That word was the beginning, the root, the strength, the mark of his whole wonderful life. His work was so blessed and fruitful, because he remained faithful to the one thing: he only lived for the will of his Lord.

There are many lessons which these words suggest. The Lord has a will, a life-plan for each of us, according to which he wishes us to live. He expects us to wait on him for the discovery of his will both in that which is universal, for all his people, as in that which he wills for each one individually. When this prayer is honest and true, it implies the whole-hearted willingness to yield ourselves and our life to the doing of that will. We may count upon an answer to such prayer, because God does not ask of his child more than he makes known as his will.

Other lessons give abundant occasion for meditation and prayer. In this chapter I desire to ask your attention to another lesson, apparently very simple, and yet of deep significance, including all the others. It is what was suggested in the opening paragraph: True conversion is nothing but a surrender to live only to do the will of God.

Do not say: But is not this a matter of course, that everyone admits? Far from it. Most Christians never have understood it. It may be that you have never yet fully grasped it. True conversion is the turning from my own will, so as never to seek to do it; the surrender of my will, with all its strengths and at all times only to seek to do what God wills.

But am I then to have no will of my own? You are indeed to have a will, the stronger the better, and to use it with all your strength, for the one great work for which God created and fitted it. That one thing was: to accept and to will what God wills. This is the image and likeness of God for which man was created, the glory and the blessedness of the life of a child of God, that he can say: the holy, heavenly, perfect will of God is my will. I have seen it and accepted it and made it my own. To will and to do with all my strength what God wills and does, this is the noblest work the will of a creature can be engaged in. In this is the very image and likeness of God: to will as he wills. We then learn to say: How wonderful, what an honour; I will always do what God wills. Or as an old saint expressed it: I am always happy, because I always have my own way; God's will and mine are always one.

This surrender to the will of God, the key of Paul's conversion and of his life, is the secret of all true conver-

sion and true Christian living. And it is because so many
have entered the Christian course without any
apprehension of God's demand that they should now
cease from all self-will, and only do his will, that they
make so little progress, that it is with them as it is written: 'They went backwards and not forwards.' They
have never understood what Scripture says of God's
children: they are 'born not of the will of man, but of
God,' 'it is not of him that willeth ... but of God which
showeth mercy,' 'of his own will begat he us, by the word
of truth.' The whole will of man, as his own power, however good and religious it may be, is shut out of the kingdom of heaven; it has to be denied and crucified; how
much more the sinful self-will. As God's will alone
brought forth the divine life in us, its whole growth and
strength are to be found in this alone. 'My meat is to do
the will of him that sent me.' The great hindrance in the
life of God in the soul is this one thing: we have not given
up our will. When once a child of God begins to see that
here lies the defect of his Christian life, there is no
deliverance until he goes back upon his conversion and
admits and confesses the one cause of failure. He did not
know how utterly evil his will was, and how entire the
renunciation of it to which he was called. When the Lord
Jesus said: 'If any man will be my disciple let him deny
himself and take up his cross,' it meant first of all, let him
deny his own will, and crucify it.

The will of God is our salvation, not only as it is willed
by him, but as it is received into our inmost being, submitted to and wrought out in our life, truly willed by us.
Because our salvation rests each moment in the saving
will of God, we can have only as much of the salvation as
we accept the will. Until this is grasped, the true reason
of our failure is not understood. As the error and the sin
are heartily acknowledged, the soul is prepared to make
a new beginning, and in the redeeming power of the
glorified Lord Jesus to say to God, Lo, I come, as it is
written in the volume of the book, not only for Christ,
but for each of his disciples: I delight to do thy will, O my

God.

If I am to turn to God in a new and full surrender to his will, it must be in a new and full trust in what Christ can do for me. Saul's question, Lord, what wilt thou have me to do? was preceded by another, out of which it was born: Who art thou, Lord? It was the vision of God in his glory, it was the personal revelation 'I am Jesus whom thou persecutest,' that wrought the mighty change, and made him yield himself so readily and so entirely to the will of his new-found Lord. We need something of the same kind. Nothing less than a new revelation of the divine authority, and the tender love of him whom we have grieved so long, but who now comes to claim and to make us the faithful servants of his will, can really enable us to say in confidence: Lord! what wilt thou have me to do? Speak Lord for thy servant will do it.

Who is ready to enter upon this path of entire devotion to the will of God, the only true Christ-life? The steps are simple.

Remember, the will of God is the revelation of his hidden divine love and blessedness, and that the only way to know and enjoy God and his love is to do his will. Say therefore boldly: I may, I will do nothing but God's will.

Believe that in answer to the prayer, Lord! what wilt thou? Jesus Christ will make known God's will day by day; and that where he teaches me to know it by his Spirit, he gives me strength to do it.

And when I have said, Lord! here am I, ready to do all thy will, let me wait upon him to reveal himself as my redeeming Lord, who with the command gives the power: his voice, his presence, his love compel a willing obedience. It is the answer to the prayer, Who art thou Lord? that prepares for the answer to the second. Lord! what wilt thou have me to do? It is the vision of Jesus fits for the doing of his will.

Lord! show thyself to me; then I can do whatever thou biddest me. In living communion with thee, I can do all things.

Chapter 10

The Man after God's Own Heart

'I have found David the son of Jesse, a man after mine own heart, which shall fulfil all my will.' Acts 13:22; 1 Samuel 13:14

Of the two expressions God uses here of David, we often hear the former: 'a man after mine own heart.' The use of the latter: 'which shall fulfil all my will,' is much less frequent. And yet it is no less important than the other. A man after mine own heart: that speaks of the deep unseen mystery of the pleasure a man can give to God in heaven. Who shall fulfil all my will: that deals with the life down here on earth which can be seen and judged by men. Let us seek and get hold of the truth that it is the man who does all God's will who is the man after his own heart. Such men God seeks: when he finds them he rejoices over them

with great joy: they are the very men he needs, men
he can trust and use. His heart, with its hidden divine
perfections, reveals itself in his will: he that seeks and
loves and does all his will is a man altogether after his
own heart: the man of absolute surrender to God's
will.

Such was David in striking contrast with Saul, the
type of the half-hearted and self-pleasing Christian.
We know what remarkable experience Saul had at the
outset of his life. The Spirit of God came upon him,
and another heart was given him and he prophesied.
There was not lacking in him a sense of humility;
when he was to be presented to the people, he hid
himself. And speedily God began to work through him
the salvation in Israel. But it was not long before self-
will began to show itself. When God sent him with the
command to destroy Amalek utterly, he did God's
work deceitfully, and under pretence of bringing sacrifices to offer to God, did his own will in the matter
of Agag and the best of the spoil. His terrible failure
was used of God, by contrast, to bring out more strik-
ingly the great truth, that the man whom God can use
to rule his people and establish his kingdom, that the
man after his own heart, who pleases him, is he of
whom he can say: he shall fulfil all my will.

After what we have already learnt of God's will,
with the place it has in the Christian life, and in preparation for a spiritual apprehension of the further
teaching of God's Word, it may be well to use these
words for the simplest possible instruction to all who
are asking the question: How can I become such a
one? What must I do that God can say of me: a man
after mine own heart, who shall fulfil all my will?

First of all, remember, you cannot attain to this by
anything you can do. No resolution, no effort, no help
you seek in prayer to strengthen your weakness, will
effect what you desire. And why not? Because you
have in you a nature wholly ruled by self-will and
wholly opposed to God's will. Nothing can delight in

God's will and actually do it, but a new and divine nature born and daily renewed in you by a divine power from above. 'The carnal mind is enmity against God,' and against his will. As entire as has been the perversion of the old nature from God and his will, must be the deliverance of the new nature from self and its will. Here is our first lesson. No desire, however honest, no purpose, however fixed, no surrender, however absolute, can make a man after God's own heart, who shall do all his will. Such a man must be born from above, and must do all he does in the power of that new divine life. A regenerate man may indeed in some things do God's will, as the fruit of the first half-unconscious workings of the Holy Spirit within him. But this is only preparatory to what God really aims at – that his child of his own free will, shall intelligently and heartily choose to do all his will. That little word 'all' is the secret of true consecration, of a life 'worthy of the Lord unto all well-pleasing', of being a man after God's own heart.

We all know what a great difference there is between a feeble child, or a sickly man, and one in full health. And so it is not enough that you just have a beginning or small measure of spiritual life; that will not enable you to do all God's will. The question is whether you are living only, and doing all, under the power of the Holy Spirit, as the strength of the new life. It is only the Spirit of God himself that can do the will of God. And the great reason why God's children do not claim, do not yield themselves by the Spirit of God to work all his will in them, is that they do not know how foolish, how helpless it is, to expect even the regenerate man to do God's will, without the direct and unceasing operation of God's Spirit. And then again, because they do not know the subtle and altogether unconquerable power of our corrupt nature, except as God himself through his Son and Spirit lives and works in the utmost recesses of our being, and inspires all its powers. If you learn the first lesson well – the secret aversion of your heart to God's will, and your complete inability to overcome or to change it, you are prepared to go on to the second.

It is this. Believe that you have a new and divine nature, expressly fitted and prepared to do all God's will, on the one condition, that you hold it in close and continual dependence upon the Holy Spirit, through whom God in Christ works in you. Jesus Christ could do nothing of himself, though he was the Son, without the Father working in him. Does it displease you to be as absolutely dependent upon God as he was? As part of your faith in Jesus Christ, believe that God works in you as in him. Believe this, however dark and feeble you feel, just as you believe, in the darkness of midnight, that the sun is shining on the other half of the world, and will in the morning rise upon you. It is this faith, with the humble, patient, dependent surrender to God which it works, that will bring you to an entirely new position and power in the doing of God's will.

In this faith, here is our third lesson, humbly but confidently give yourself up to God to do all his will. Give yourself to him, as a loving Father, so that you do not take his commands as a mere law, but as a loving will – the will of the Father, made known in the loving fellowship by himself to yourself. Look at God's will as one great whole – the relation of his loving purpose with man and with you. Set yourself now resolutely, in the faith of the Holy Spirit's working in you, to make it your own business every day to do all God's will. Then again, bow yourself in the deepest humility and impotence to wait on God to work in you. The humility that bows in deep grief at the enmity of the evil nature against God's will in confession of the impotence of the regenerate nature of itself to do that will, in the dependence of a chidlike waiting on God for him to work his will in you, will be a new entrance into the kingdom of heaven. The Christian life will become something quite new to you under the

power of these great truths: your utter and ever-abid-
ing impotence to do God's will, even as a regenerate
man, without the unceasing work of the Holy Spirit:
your divine and complete sufficiency in Christ for all
that the Father asks of you when he calls you to be a
man after his own heart, who shall do all his will.

Chapter 11

The Will of the Lord be Done

'And when Paul would not be persuaded, we ceased, saying: The will of the Lord be done.'
Acts 21:14

Paul was at Caesarea, on his way to Jerusalem. Agabus, a prophet, had said by the Holy Spirit that Paul would there be bound, and delivered into the hands of the Gentiles. Paul's friends besought him not to go up. In his answer he spoke the noble words: I am ready not to be bound only, but also to die at Jerusalem for the name of the Lord Jesus. When they heard this, they said: The will of the Lord be done. It was no longer a question of Jews or Gentiles, not even of the life or death of Paul; if it was to be, they would accept it as the will of God. The story teaches us the wisdom, the duty, the blessing of accepting disappointing or trail that cannot be averted, as

God's will, and so turning what naturally would cause sorrow or anger into an occasion of holy resignation and humble worship of God in his sovereign wisdom and power.

There is a twofold will of God: the will of approval and the will of permission. In the former we see what he desires or ordains as right and good. The latter includes all that happens in the world either as the result of natural law and second causes, or as the work of ungodly men and evil spirits. To admit that what God's will directly appoints is good is comparatively easy. But to recognise his will in all the evil that comes to us or around us from evil men, is a truth many a believer never accepts. It is one of the most blessed lessons anyone can learn to see that no possible trouble can ever come to us, that is not for us in very deed the will of our Father. Though Judas, and Caiaphas, and Pilate seemed against God's holy and righteous will in the death of Jesus, the suffering and death they caused him he accepted as the will of God, the cup the Father gave him. The sin of those who persecute or hurt a child of God is not his will, and yet the suffering caused, with all its consequences, is to them God's will. As this is seen the believer turns his eyes from the human cause to the heavenly Father's will, and finds that suffering becomes a blessing, and that no power on earth or in hell can rob the soul of the perfect rest there is in God's blessed will. The place of trial becomes the place of blessing. Let us see what is needed to secure this.

1. In time of trial let me say at once: Here I am by the will of God, in the very place God has chosen for me. Whether the trial comes from the hatred of an enemy, or the wrong of a friend, through my own fault or in the course of God's more direct Providence, I may be sure, and ought therefore heartily to consent to it, that the difficulty or distress in which I am is the will of God concerning me. Whether it be some great trial, or some petty annoyance, whether a temporary grief or some long continued cause of weariness or irritation, be sure

that the secret of peace and rest is to say: This trouble is what God wills for me. It is this that lifts me from man to God and his will. To that will I have yielded myself. In that will I rest. The will of theLord be done.

2. This prepares the soul to say with confidence: God, who has brought me into this trouble, will assuredly give the grace to bear it aright. The grace that is needed to bear suffering as God would have his child do it, so as to glorify him in it, must come from him. The quiet submission, the childlike trust, the living entrance into and union with his will, he will work in the soul that adoringly says: The will of the Lord be done. All the promises of the holy Scripture, with all the comfort they afford in the assurance of God's presence and help in trouble, depend for their fulfilment on this one condition, that the soul gives itself up to the will of God. Then can we prove that God's will is love and blessing. The more willingly I say, God brought me here, the more confidently I can say, he has charge and cares for me.

3. We shall then be led farther on to the assurance: God himself will teach me the lesson for which he sent the trial. This is something more than the trust, and peace, and surrender we have just been speaking of. They keep us from grieving God or vexing ourselves in the school of affliction. But beyond these graces God has special lessons for every child whom he leads aside in his loving chastisement. He wants to cure us permanently of our self-will and our worldliness, to waken us into the true imitation of the humility and the self-sacrifice of his Son, to draw us into full fellowship with him who made us for his divine indwelling and operation within us, to fit us to live lives of blessing to others. These lessons are often sadly missed by those who suffer much. And those who try to learn them often feel how greatly they have failed. It is because we do not believe; the Father, who brought me into this place of trial, will himself teach the lesson he would have me learn and work all the grace he would see in me. The will of the Lord be done, includes not only the trial itself but all that God meant by it, and

has undertaken to work out in the willing, waiting, soul.

4. When thus we have entered into living union with the Father through his will, we shall not fear to say: God's will, which brought me here, can in his way and time, bring me out again. With many children of God the desire for deliverance from trouble is the first, if not even the only, thought. This should not be so. Suffering is not natural to us; we are at liberty to call upon God for deliverance in the day of trouble. But it is not for this alone the heart must turn to God. The first desire must be that God may be glorified in loving submission, and childlike teachableness: that his will in all it means and aims at with the trial may be done. It is when, in this its true and full meaning, the prayer: The will of the Lord be done, rises from the heart, that the burden may be taken away without our being the losers, and that the deliverance may bring as much glory to God in our holy devotion as the suffering could have done. The union with God's will will teach us how to look to it in the right spirit for help.

What a privilege that the darkest trials, the bitterest sorrows, as well as the smaller disappointments or the passing fears of life, can all help to unite me more perfectly with the will of my God. By his grace I will seek to live every day, amid tears of sorrow and songs of joy, in quiet submission or in triumphant faith, as they do in heaven, with the one word in the heart: The will of the Lord be done. It is this that gives heaven on earth.

Chapter 12

Of Knowing God's Will

'And ... Ananias ... said, The God of our fathers hath chosen thee, that thou shouldest know his will, and see that Just One, and shouldest hear the voice of his mouth.'
Acts 22:12,14

When Saul said, Lord! what wilt thou have me to do? the reference was to personal immediate duty. When Ananias, after three days, spoke of his call from God 'to know his will,' the thought was a much larger one. Saul had been prepared by God as his chosen vessel, to whom he could entrust 'the mystery of his will,' 'the mystery of Christ', 'which from the beginning of the world had been hid in God', 'that the Gentiles should be fellowheirs, and of the same body, and partakers of his promise in Christ by the gospel' (Eph.1:9; 3:3–9).

I have previously spoken of the need of not confining our knowledge of God's will to the commands and promises which have special reference to ourselves. All God's children are called to enlarge their hearts, to take a personal interest in the great work God is seeking to carry out in the world, and so to be ready to take their part in the fulfilment of his purpose – the winning back of the world to him, to be the kingdom of his Son.

In studying Paul's surrender to Christ's will in conversion, we saw how closely that was linked to his vision of the Lord in heaven. Here we find the same connection: 'Appointed to know his will, and see that Just One.' The mystery of God's will is the mystery of Christ: to know the will is inseparable from knowing the Just One, who puts away sin, and is to rule in righteousness on the earth. In the life and writings of Paul we see how firmly he holds the two truths together. It is ever 'Jesus Christ our Lord ... by whom we have received grace and apostleship, for obedience to the faith among all nations, for his name.' As one who had seen and heard him, Paul's gospel was ever a personal witness. He never preached the will of God as a doctrine, or a decree, or even as a revelation, apart from the living person of that Lord Jesus in whom that will had received all its riches and blessings, and in personal contact with whom alone its salvation could be realised. To know the will, and to see the Just One, let these ever be inseparable. The living Christ himself can alone fit us to know and do the will of God. To know the will and not see the Just One would make it a new law of Moses, a burden heavy to be borne. To see him is to know the will in the light of God's love, to know it in divine beauty and perfection, and to receive the power to do it.

All that God did in Paul was 'for an ensample unto them which should hereafter believe.' Like him, and through him, each of us is called, in our measure, to know this larger will of God, his purpose for all men, that the gospel should be preached to every creature. There is no sadder proof of how little it is understood or preached that, just as Christ, so his church is only in the world to carry out this divine will, than the lack, in the great majority of Christians, of anything like enthusiastic devotion to the cause of missions. Even among those who do give them a measure of support, there is so little sense of the overwhelming prominence which ought to be given to this will of God. It is not one command among others. It is the one thing in which the will of the Father includes everything. That all men should know and honour Christ. It is the one thing for which the church exists, to be a light of them that are in darkness. It is the one thing by which a child of God can prove that he lives not unto himself but unto him that died for him and rose again. It is the one truth that above all else needs to be restored to its place, and which assuredly will bring the revival of every other truth of the spiritual life as its necessary condition. This is in very deed the will of God, that the church as the body of Christ, and every believer as its member, is to seek first, absolutely first, the kingdom of God, and that his will be done throughout the earth as in heaven.

And what can be the reason, if this be the will of God, that the church has so little apprehended or fulfilled it? If Paul was divinely illuminated to know that will, and to make it known to the church, how is it that it has so little possessed the church of Christ? The answer is not far to seek. Just as in Paul this will of God needed a very special spiritual revelation, so still. It is easy, when once a truth has been seen and pointed out by spiritual men, for other Christians to see and accept it too. And yet it may be an article of mental belief, that does not really, through living faith, master and possess the heart. The will of God is a living spiritual energy; we do not know that will truly until it has entered and filled our will. As love alone can meet love, and heart alone touch heart, so will alone can apprehend will. Anything less is but a mental image, a conception of the truth, not the thing itself in its reality and power. And so a great deal of the missionary interest of our day proves, by the feeble hold it has, and the little sacrifice there is made for it, and the need of continual appeal to minor motives, that the knowledge of this mystery of God's will is not held in the power of the Spirit.

Paul speaks of 'the riches of the glory of this mystery among the Gentiles; which is Christ in you, the hope of glory.' It is only as the mystery of Christ in us, the experience of an indwelling Christ is truly known, that the glory of the mystery will be seen to be this, that it is the will of God for all the Gentiles. The more truly I know by the Spirit what it is to have Christ in me, the more I shall long and labour that it may be Christ in all.

'God hath chosen thee, that thou shouldest know his will, and see that Just One, and shouldest hear the voice of his mouth. For thou shalt be his witness unto all men of what thou hast seen and heard.' God gave Paul as an example; in your measure this word is for you too, my reader. Do believe that in this mystery of God's will for the Gentiles the glory of God, of Christ, of the church, of every believer is centred. All God's wisdom and power, his holiness and love and faithfulness meet in it. And you are appointed – what a privilege – to know his will, and have it possess you, and use you as its instrument and messenger. Fear not to yield thyself utterly to it, a living sacrifice. 'Chosen to know his will, and (here is your strength) to see that Just One,' who himself wrought that will and now works mightily in all who see him, and receive him as their Lord who dwells in them. Oh, cast yourself into this mighty stream of divine love – the will of God for the salvation of the ends of the earth.

Chapter 13

God Working out His Own Will

'Being predestinated according to the purpose of him who worketh all things after the counsel of his own will.' Ephesians 1:11

In the epistle to the Ephesians we have three passages concerning the will of God. The first, in chapter 1, points us back to the eternal mystery of that will in God, and tells us how as God purposed it in himself, so he himself works it all out. The second, in chapter 5, calls us to seek to understand what the will of God is. The third, in chapter 6, brings us down into practical life, and teaches us how the most common drudgery of daily duty may all be done as the will of God. As in the heights of heaven and of eternity, so down into the conduct and the heart of the humblest Christian the will of God claims supreme authority. Let us begin and study it in its origin and work before the foundation of the world.

Paul writes in Ephesians 1:5–11 of God having 'predestinated us unto the adoption of children by Jesus Christ to himself, according to the good pleasure of his will … according to the riches of his grace; wherein he hath abounded us … having made known unto us the mystery of his will, according to his good pleasure which he hath purposed in himself … in whom also we have obtained an inheritance, being predestinated according to the purpose of him who worketh all things after the counsel of his own will.' Each expression has its significance. The good pleasure of his will – that means the absolute liberty of God, the perfection of whose will knows no higher reason than that it so pleased him. The mystery of his will – that suggests that it was hidden in God, that we can only know as much of it as he reveals, and that even what he reveals still has its mystery beyond our comprehension. The purpose of his will – that refers to the great plan or scheme to be carried out which his holy will formed for itself. And the counsel of his will reminds us of the divine 'wisdom and prudence' (v 8) holding counsel with itself and ordering all so as to prove that his good pleasure is indeed all that is most right and good and perfect. In the secret depths of God's will and its predestinating purpose lies hidden the salvation of his church and of every member of it.

'Being predestinated according to the purpose of him who worketh all things after the counsel of his own will.' What God has willed, he also himself works out. The counsel of his will is too high and holy; none but he can work it out. The will is a working power, a determination to act, even a man who really wills a thing seeks to overcome every obstacle to that will being realised. We need, as we study and worship the will of God, to give full scope to the conviction that God himself works out all things after the counsel of his will. The eternal purpose is what guides all his work: all that the eternal purpose fixed must and will be wrought by himself. This faith will teach us some most precious lessons.

It inspires the assurance that God's purpose will be performed. We are so apt to look to ourselves and our feebleness, to men and to circumstances, and by these to measure what appears possible. We need to remember that God's sovereign will is a power that will as much in the great whole as in the minutest detail infallibly secure the fulfilment of his plans. Whether in our own heart and life, or in the service of his kingdom in which we take part, we need definitely to know him as the 'God who worketh all in all.' We speak of man's relationship to God as that of co-operation. But human co-operation implies divine operation – the latter as unceasing and continuous as the former, even proceeding and drawing it forth. All feebleness in the divine life, all failure in spiritual work, is owing to this one thing: we do not make room to do the divine will without the living faith in him who himself worketh all things after the counsel of his will.

This faith will teach us to live and work in entire dependence on God's working. It will waken and strengthen us in that root of all true Christian virtue, humility. It is through this that the angels kept their first estate – they live in entire dependence upon God's willing and working in them. It was for this that the Son assumed the robe of creaturehood, to teach us that the life and glory of the creature consists in every moment receiving from God what we are to be, to will or to do. He did nothing of himself, but as he heard so he spake. The connection between God and us is to be one of never ceasing receptivity, God every moment imparting the life and strength we need. As we learn to know God thus, we shall fear nothing so much as taking his place, by our work hindering his, and so under the guise of doing his will making it impossible for him to do it. Oh, let us in deep humility and reverence worship and wait on the God who worketh all things after the counsel of his will.

This faith will lead us to true diligence in God's service

through the blessed confidence of being indeed able to do all his will because what he wills he works himself. At first sight it appears as if this entire unceasing dependence upon God will hinder us in our work. That is only as long as we do not understand or believe it fully. But to the upright, who wait on God, light will arise. It will be with them even as with the truth of faith without works for justification. At first it appears as if this would discourage good works in the believer. But as we indeed give ourselves away to the blessed truth of faith without works for acceptance, we find that it is this very faith that is most abundant in producing good works as its fruit. Even so, as we accept fully the truth of which we were afraid at first sight, that we can do nothing of ourselves, and that God must do all, we shall experience that the most absolute and unceasing dependence is the secret of the most effective service. As works before faith only hinder, while faith without works is most fruitful of works, so the attempt to work without the fullest and most entire dependence upon God leads to continual failure, until ceasing from ourselves and our works has brought us to yield ourselves unreservedly to God's working, there to learn what it means to say: 'I also labour, striving according to his working, which worketh in me mightily.' The faith of our entire impotence and dependence upon God becomes the power for our highest activity.

'Predestinated according to the purpose of him who worketh all things after the counsel of his own will.' Believer, the purpose accordingly (and for which you have predestined) is that of a God who works all things after the counsel of his will. Let every thought of the will of God be accompanied by the faith that he is a God who himself works all things that he wills. All goodness and power are his, to be received direct from him alone through Christ Jesus. Worship him with a holy fear, lest, like Martha, you grieve your Lord by your much serving, instead of waiting, like Mary, for what he can work in you. What God hath joined together let no man put asunder: God working his will in man by the Holy Spirit; man working the will God has wrought in man in secret into daily life and duty.

Chapter 14

Understanding the Will of God

'Be not foolish, but understand what the will of the Lord is.' Ephesians 5:17

In the preceding chapter I spoke of the three passages in this epistle on the will of God. The first lifted us up into the eternal glory, to worship God, of whose glory that will is the revelation, and who himself works it out in time. The last will lead down to the hut and the burden of the slave, and show us how even there, in the most commonplace everyday life, the will of God may be done on earth as in heaven. Our present subject stands between the two, as the indispensable link. It is only as I know the will of God, both in the place it has in his life, and is to have in mine, that I can appreciate the blessedness and fulfil the duty of ever only doing the will of the Father. It is the danger of neglecting the careful study to know all that God's will implies, that makes Paul write, 'Be not foolish, but understand what the will of the Lord is.'

'Be not foolish'. In our conceit that, with our Christian education, our commonsense, our daily Bible reading, we know well enough what God's will must be, we prove that we are as fools, without the wisdom of God guiding us. 'Let no man deceive himself. If any man thinketh that he is wise in this world, let him become a fool, that he may be wise. If any man thinketh he knoweth anything, he knoweth nothing yet as he ought to know.' Let us beware of the folly of thinking we know the will of God. Let us become fools indeed, in the sense of our great ignorance, and seek the divine teaching which alone can rightly reveal the divine will.

'Be not foolish, but understand what the will of the Lord is.' To understand a thing means, not only to know its outward form, but something of its true nature, its inner meaning and working. It is only as the believer seeks a spiritual insight into God's will, that the doing of it will become the heavenly joy it is meant to be. Let us consider what are some of the chief elements of the true understanding of God's will.

Think of it, first of all, in connection with God himself. His will is the power by which he determined what he is to do, and what is to be done by his creatures. In that will all his goodness and wisdom, love and power are revealed; the knowledge of that will open to the creature the very heart of God. In the surrender to and worship of that will angels and men rise into living fellowship with God. Over the carrying out of that will God himself watches. What the divine wisdom has planned, divine power will perform. Never for a moment can the will of God be separated from God himself; if you would understand that will, never think of it but as the symbol of the presence of the living God himself. Always seek to see God in his will.

Think of it then as made known in his Word. The words of holy Scripture for the most part are plain and simple, so as to be understood of all. And yet, because they contain the mystery of divine wisdom, the understanding of the meaning of the words does not at all ensure the real spiritual understanding or apprehension of God's will. The words need to be taken into the heart, into the faith and love and obedience of man's whole being, and God's divine working through them needs to be waited for, before we can fully understand God's will. The very same Spirit which, having searched the deep things of God, inspired by the Word, must give him light and faith in the depths of our heart too, if the will of God is really to become our will. Without this all our knowledge is merely intellectual and superficial. It is only God working his will into our will, and our will accepting it heartily, that can fit us to understand what the will of the Lord is. The will, the intense desire to do all God's will, is the secret of knowing it.

Think of that will especially as embodied in Christ Jesus. He is the Word of God, the visible image of the hidden glory of God's will. As man, he came to show us how it is the calling and the blessedness of the creature to give itself up wholly to the will of God, and do nothing of itself, and how it may count most confidently on God himself working in it both to will and to do all his will. As our Redeemer, he died to deliver us from our own will, and now leads us in the path of dying to self, to live and do God's will alone. Any attempt to understand the will of God, apart from its intimate union with the Son of God our Saviour, ends in foolishness. It is in living union with Jesus alone, that either light or strength for knowing and doing the Father's will can come.

Understand what the will of the Lord is. Think of its claim on your whole life. You cannot attempt fully to yield to or rejoice in that claim until you see that it rests in the New Testament upon the fact that the renewed will is a ray of the divine will itself, taking possession of you, of your inner being, and from within enabling you to love God's will as wholly and as naturally as you formerly loved your self-will. The three-in-one God has begun his own life in you; his will and the power that works it out are in you; in the faith of that admit heartily the claim of God's will to have complete dominion. See that, and say there is to be nothing in your life that is not to be under the control, or rather the inspiration of God's will. In the faith of this living root of God's will possessing you, your will and his inextricably intertwined, look upon the Word with its exceeding breadth covering every possible position, and upon your daily life with its innumerable needs and duties, and understand how the will of God can be carried out through all. 'Created in Christ Jesus unto good works, which God hath before ordained that we should walk in them', – you can count upon the Holy Spirit to lead you into all God's perfect will.

Understand what the will of the Lord is. To sum up all, think of God's will not only as having come forth from an infinite love, as revealed and embodied in the written and the eternal Word, as claiming your whole life down to its minutest details, but, above all, as the promise of what God himself will work in you. Understand the will of God is so divine, and holy, and perfect, only God himself can work it. You can only work it as he works it in you by his Holy Spirit. As your faith in God's working all his will in you becomes stronger and more unceasing and more joyfully confident, the more will you know that it is possible for you to do that will. 'According to your faith be it unto you', will in this also be made true in you. Standing in the full light of the eternal love as it shines on you from heaven, you will find that light is cast upon the whole of the Word and of life. And you will then begin to understand what the will of the Lord is. The most wonderful, beautiful, blessed thing in the universe. The one thing to be sought and loved, to be done or suffered. The one thing worth living and dying for.

Chapter 15

Doing
the Will of God
from the Heart

*'Servants, be obedient to them that are your
masters ... in singleness of your heart, as unto
Christ; Not with eyeservice, as men-pleasers;
but as the servants of Christ, doing the will of
God from the heart; With good will doing
service, as to the Lord, and not to men.'*
Ephesians 6:5–7

The importance of the teaching these words contain can
hardly be overrated. They tell us that not only when we
are fulfilling some direct command, but equally when we
are doing our common daily work, all is to be done, may
be done, as the will of God. They tell us that this cannot

be done except as it is done in singleness of heart, and from the heart, with the joyful and loving consent of our whole being. They tell us too that the strength thus to act is to be found in doing all as in Christ's presence and unto him. They teach us too how the most common daily life with its drudgery or even its oppression may be transfigured into the work of heaven – doing the will of God.

The passage derives special force from the fact that it was addressed to slaves. At that time almost all servants were slaves, entirely, even with their life, at the disposal of their masters, and with no rights in law. Many of the early Christians were slaves, of the base and despised whom God had chosen. Their servitude was often harsh and thankless, and the very liberty and brotherhood which the Gospel preached would only make some of them feel all the more the bondage they endured. To such Paul writes, to be obedient to their masters, as unto Christ, and to perform all their service as the will of God from the heart. If this was expected of these slaves, just come out of heathenism, in circumstances of such difficulty, it is surely time that our Christianity had learned the lesson that everything we do, even the compulsory or ill-requited service of a hard master, is to be done as the will of God.

And how can this disposition be attained? Only in one way. By heartily accepting any position into which providence brings us as God's will for us. Then the work we have to do in that position will be God's will for us. In our opening chapter we saw that one of the first lessons in the Christian life is to accept every trouble that comes to us from the mistakes of ourselves or others, or the trial of circumstances, as God's appointment. His providence is his will for us. This alone can prevent the irritation and anger and fretfulness that so often embitters life, and clouds the sense of God's favour. Nothing under heaven can then disturb our faith or peace: to see God in all gives rest and hope. Every work we have to perform, however unpleasant, however unjust or ill-rewarded, becomes, as long as God allows it, his will for us. To do it as much makes it easy and makes it holy, a well-pleasing sacrifice. And if this be true of the work of a slave, much more does it hold good of all the duties of daily life. In housekeeping and business, in all the thousandfold work or service in earning a livelihood or fulfilling a calling – everything must, may be done as the will of God.

The thought at once suggests itself of this demand being too high and hard. Who can always be remembering, with so much to occupy and disturb, that this common work is all God's will? There is only one way to succeed in doing this, and that is to do the work 'in singleness of heart' from the heart. The heart means desire, will, love, delight, joy. What we do from the heart is a pleasure. The only religion that satisfied God is that of the heart; that is why he asks us to love him with the whole heart. As long as we only take God's will as a law that we are obliged to obey, for our own safety and happiness, or to prove our faith and gratitude, the doing of it is a burden. But when we take it into our heart as a thing we delight in, and cannot have too much of, as what we have given our life up to, everything is welcome that gives us an opportunity for doing more of that blessed will, for keeping our devotion to it unbroken.

'Doing the will of God from the heart.' God not only asks the heart: he has promised to put his law into our heart. God wants the heart, and nothing less can please him. He has therefore made provision for securing it. He sends forth the spirit of his Son into our heart. Let us believe in the Holy Spirit dwelling in us, and working the love of God. Let us in that faith worship and give ourselves away to 'the beautiful, sweet will of God', and cherish it as our choicest treasure and chief desire. As it gets possession of the heart, and opens itself in it, the heart that has learnt to adore its glory in God will learn to welcome every trace of it on earth, and we shall find ourselves doing the hardest service in singleness of heart, with the heart only set upon pleasing God, in very deed doing the will of God from the heart.

Our text tells us one thing more – how the doing the will of God will always be connected with the presence of Christ. The will of God and the Son of God are inseparable. Jesus is the will of God. He did it. He works that will from heaven. His great work as Saviour is to secure our doing it. And so Paul writes to the slaves: 'be obedient to your masters ... as unto Christ; Not with eyeservice, as men-pleasers, but as the servants of Christ ... With good will doing service, as unto the Lord.' Here we have the thrice-repeated thought that in the daily drudgery the animating motive is to be that it is a service rendered to the Lord we love. His presence and his pleasure are to be our inspiration. The poor slave could understand that. The eye of the slave – his master, with the fear of displeasing him, spurred on to continuous effort. The presence of Jesus Christ, the sense of being his servant, the bondslave of his love, the glory of pleasing him, can as unceasingly fill the heart, and carry you through all the day, doing work for men, as servants of Christ: the presence of Christ fits us for this. He knows what the difficulties and temptations are in the way of always doing God's will. He knows how the victory can be obtained, and the will of God always be done. He lives to secure to us the strength and the victory. If we give ourselves to nothing less than to be wholly his servants in ever doing God's will alone, if we trust him to maintain his own presence in us all the day, we can know the joy of his service in his strength.

'Doing the will of God from the heart.' Let God, let Jesus Christ, God's Son, let God's love, have the heart, the whole heart, and nothing less, and God's will will be done by us on earth, as it is in heaven. God himself will work it in us, and amid all the changing circumstances of life there will be one thing that never changes – our place of rest in the centre of God's will.

Chapter 16

Knowing and Not Doing

'Behold, thou art called a Jew ... and makest thy boast of God, And knowest his will ... and art confident that thou thyself art a guide of the blind ... Thou therefore which teachest another, teachest thou not thyself? thou that preachest a man should not steal, dost thou steal? Romans 2:17–21

In chapter 1 of this epistle we have the terrible unrighteousness of the heathen, with its consequent darkness, portrayed. In chapter 2, the self-righteousness of the Jews, with the fatal delusion that rests in the knowing of God's will without doing it. Men gloried in God and made their boast of Israel's having had a divine revelation, and being the depository of God's will, and yet never thought of the folly of not doing that will. It is the same evil against which Christ warned when he said: 'Not every one that saith unto me, Lord, Lord, shall enter into the kingdom of heaven; but he that doeth the will of my Father which is in heaven.' The subject of this chapter is the terrible possibility of glorying in God and delighting in the study and the knowledge of his will, and yet not doing it. Let us try and discover the cause of this sad phenomenon, as it is as frequent in the Christian church as in Israel. That will lead us to see what its cure must be. Let us bring our own life into the full light of scriptural teaching, and find out whether the doing of God's will has really that supreme place in our thought and conduct which it has in the mind of God and the teaching of Christ.

One would say that from the very nature of the thing every Christian would know that doing God's will is the very essence of true religion. Whether we regard him as Creator or Lawgiver, as Father or Redeemer, we cannot but admit that we cannot honour or please, cannot fulfil our relationship to him, without living according to his will. Whether we think of the escape from the power of sin, or the walk in his fellowship and love, or the participation in the happiness of his service, here or hereafter, everything points to the doing of God's will as the only possible way of really living in the enjoyment of salvation. What can be the reason that so many Christians have never known that doing God's will is the very first duty of the Christian's life, indispensable to its health and safety?

With many the cause is an entire misapprehension of the nature of salvation. They have misunderstood God's glorious gospel. They heard that God justifies the ungodly, of free grace, without any works of righteousness he ever had done or needed to do to secure God's favour. They heard right. But they understood wrong. They were content to believe in the pardon of sin, and deliverance from punishment, and never saw that salvation means restoration to the love and fellowship of God, to the honour and blessedness of a walk in obedience to his will. Content with being saved from guilt, they never thought that being saved from the doing of sin is the real proof of the power of salvation, and the real entrance upon a life in the likeness and holiness of God. The entire reasonableness, the unspeakable blessedness, the indispensable necessity, the supreme obligation of seeking and loving to do God's will as it is done in heaven, has never dawned upon them. Entirely to give up their own will in order to follow and carry out God's will has never become an article of their creed. They are content with the traditional, conventional view of Christian duty, but never thought that all that is known of God's will, must at once be done.

With others the cause of failure in doing God's will is a misapprehension as to the power of salvation. They believe that God's law is unchangeable in its demands, and that it is their bounden duty to obey it perfectly. They have learnt from Scripture and experience how utterly impotent they are to fulfil its claims. They have never understood how in the New Testament the law of God with its inexorable demand and condemnation becomes transformed into the will of God, which does not mean mere demand but actual living power. They know now what it means: Ye are not under the law, with its impotence, but under grace, with its omnipotence, working in you all that it asks. They are held in bondage of the legal spirit, and do not believe that it is possible to live a life in the will of God. They admire and delight in a promise such as 'my grace is sufficient for thee, my strength is made perfect in weakness', or a testimony: I can do all things through Christ which strengtheneth me, but dare not expect their fulfilment in their own doing of God's will. They do not think it possible always to be doing God's will.

There are still others who believe both in the obligation and the possibility, and yet complain of continual failure. The reason is with them very much misapprehension as to the knowledge of God's will. They study God's Word very earnestly to find out God's will, and yet fail to find with that knowledge the strength to perform. They know not that it is only where the light of the Holy Spirit shows God's will, that his strength will work it in us. The will of God, discovered and accepted by our human wisdom, must be obeyed by our human strength. The humble, childlike spirit that believe that the Father will by his Spirit show us what he wants us to do, will receive grace also to believe that for what the Father wants and shows, he will give the needed strength. As we see that it is not enough for us to have the Word and out of that take what we think we ought to do, but wait on God for guidance, to know what he would have us to do, we shall learn that to be taught God's will by his Spirit, is half the secret of being strengthened by him to do it.

Believer, Jesus Christ your Saviour came to do the will of God and to enable you to do it too. Do you know him as your Owner, who claims to have thy whole being, with every power and every moment? Have you acknowledged his ownership, and yielded yourself wholly to live only as he would have you? Have you, in the faith of his strength, made this surrender, and believed that by his Holy Spirit he seals and maintains it? Then, be not afraid to believe that he will show you all God's will for you and fit you for doing it. Believe that, morning by morning, he will open your ear to hear his voice, and that to the meek and lonely of heart he will give God's light and God's strength for all God's will.

Chapter 17

The Renewed Mind Proving God's Will

*'Be not conformed to this world: but be ye
transformed by the renewing of your mind,
that ye may prove what is that good, and
acceptable, and perfect, will of God.'*
Romans 12:2

With the first verse of Romans 12 the practical part of the
epistle begins with Paul's imploring believers to present
their bodies a living sacrifice, holy, acceptable to God.
In verse 2 there follows the call to these God-devoted
men, if their sacrifice is indeed to be acceptable to God,
to prove, that is, to find out and show, what is the acceptable will of God. He who would live as an acceptable sacrifice must live in the acceptable will of God. The one
acceptable sacrifice is the doing of the acceptable will.
To live in the will of God is the one and only thing that

can make us well-pleasing to him. The only object and proof of true consecration is doing the will of God.

The three adjectives Paul uses, the good, and acceptable, and perfect will of God, indicate three stages in our proving and knowing the will of God. The first refers to our discerning between good and evil, and our accepting what we know of God's will as indeed good. The second points to our knowledge of God's will in special relation to ourselves. The will of God is not the same for all his children; as we find out what is specially the will of God for ourselves, we know that what we do is actually acceptable, well-pleasing to him. The third word, perfect, tells us that we may not rest content with what we already know and do of God's will; this is only a beginning; we must press on to stand perfect in all the will of God. To know and accept the will of God as good, is the first step, is good. To know it in our personal relationship to him as well-pleasing, is better. To know the perfect will of God is best of all, the true aim of the full Christian life. So we can prove and know for ourselves, so we can prove to men, what is the good, and acceptable, and perfect will of God. So we yield our bodies an acceptable sacrifice. On the first great call of the epistle: 'live wholly as sacrifices to God', follows at once the second as its complement: 'live only to do the will of God'.

Between these two commands there are inserted a warning and an exhortation: 'be not conformed to this world' – that is the warning against your first and greatest danger: 'be ye transformed by the renewing of your mind': the exhortation reveals the path and the strength in which it becomes possible to stand perfect in all the will of God.

Would you indeed know and do God's will, listen to the warning: 'be not conformed to this world.' 'The friendship of the world is enmity with God.' Its root principle, that by which it became a 'world which lieth in wickedness', was the rejection of the will of God. The world may acknowledge a God; but it cannot and will not do his will. It cannot by its very nature do anything but its own will. We are by nature of the world. We are still in it, and ever in danger of being under its influence. After our regeneration the secret, subtle atmosphere with which it surrounds us, and with which the flesh is in alliance, hinders thousands of Christians from seeking a life of true and full devotion to the will of God. Unless with our whole heart we reject its principles, its pleasures, its pursuits, we gradually lose the spiritual capacity of delighting in and performing God's will. Unless we come out from the world, where self-will and self-pleasing rules, we never can live the life in which the believer only seeks to be a sacrifice well-pleasing to God, and to prove the well-pleasing will of God. Do let us believe it – the great cause of failure in doing the will of God is simply – a worldly spirit. Therefore, beware: 'be not conformed to this world.'

The negative, not being fashioned according to the world, must be accompanied by the positive: 'but be ye transformed by the renewing of your mind.' The renewal in regeneration, once for all, must be followed up by the continual renewing of the Holy Spirit. 'Be renewed in the spirit of your mind.' He saved us, by the washing of regeneration, and renewing of the Holy Ghost.' The only power that can enable us to live as living, holy, acceptable sacrifices, that can fit us truly to delight in doing the will of God. The attempt to do the will of God with a heart that does not daily seek and find the renewing in the spirit of the mind of the Holy Spirit, must end in failure. It is only a healthy man can do a healthy man's work. It is only a spiritual man who can walk in the spiritual path of obedience to all God's will.

I ask you, beloved believer, to pause and take in the lessons we have been finding. To prove what is the good and acceptable will of God is the calling and the privilege of every believer. It is impossible to fulfil this calling, except as we know that we have definitely yielded ourselves to live as holy sacrifices, well-pleasing to God in everything. The one great hindrance to this is a worldly spirit in conformity to the dispositions and habits of the men of the world. The only power that can overcome this danger is that of the Holy Spirit: to be daily transformed by the renewing of our mind gives the spiritual capacity to know, to love, to do all God's will.

If you find that you are not yet living this life, rest not till you know and receive the same. If it is because you have never definitely and finally accepted God's will as your life, do so now. If it be that you have never presented yourself a living sacrifice – come at once, and yield to God's claim! By the mercies of God, I beseech you: give up yourself to the God who redeemed you. If you have done so but failed, because you never knew how much there was of the world in you – begin at once to live the life of not being fashioned according to the world, but being transformed by the renewing of the Holy Spirit.

Take courage, my Christian friend! The eternal spirit through whom Christ said 'I delight to do thy will', and offered himself a sacrifice unto God, dwells in you. Yield yourself as a sacrifice for him to consume. Believe and receive his daily renewing; he will fit you for proving all the perfect will of God.

Chapter 18

According to the Will of God

'Our Lord Jesus Christ, Who gave himself for our sins, that he might deliver us from this present evil world, according to the will of God and our Father.' Galatians 1:3–4

Paul always carried with him a very deep sense of the will of God as the source and the rule of all things. In five of the epistles he speaks of himself as an apostle, 'through the will of God'. The thought of God's will dominated his whole ministry, inspiring at once devotion and obedience, dependence and perfect confidence. He loved to think of God's will working out its purpose through him. Of his intention to visit Rome he speaks more than once as coming to them 'by the will of God.' Of the Macedonians giving themselves first to the Lord and then to him, he says too that it was 'by the will of God'. And so here, in speaking of the work of God's Son in our redemption, he shows how its chief characteristic is that it was 'according to the will of God.' Whether in his own life, or in the grace manifested in his converts, or in the work of our Lord Jesus, salvation is to him the will of God manifesting itself and working out his purpose.

The expression he uses in regard to Christ's work is a somewhat unusual and remarkable one. 'He gave himself for our sins that he might deliver us out of this present evil world, according to the will of our God and Father.' It gives us a new aspect of the Father's will as revealed in Christ's death. In our last meditation (Rom 12:2) we saw how, in the spiritual life, being conformed to the world was the first great danger of the consecrated soul, and being transformed out of it into newness of life the only way to a life in the good and perfect will of God. Here we discover the deepest root of that teaching. The whole will of God in Christ's death had this one object – to deliver us from this present evil world. The spirit of the world and the will of God are diametrically opposite: the will of God demands, and promises, and works entire deliverance from it. If we would know the will of God aright and live in it and according to it, we must come out and be entirely separate from all that is of this present evil world. That alone is true and full salvation.

'This present evil world.' And was not this world created by God? And is it all so entirely evil as to deserve the name 'this evil world', and to need the Son of God to deliver us from it? Yes. Scripture teaches that with the entrance of sin into the world it came into the power of the prince of evil. When in Adam's fall, Satan obtained power over him, the world, over which he was to have been king, fell with him, and Satan became the god of this world, and all men born into it. The world is now an organised kingdom of evil, ruled by the god, animated by the spirit of the world. 'The whole world lieth in wickedness.' The development of evil, now in its slow growth, then in its sudden outbreaks, is no blind evolution, but the result of a deliberate systematic war of an intelligent power of evil against the rule of God. Whether in the grossest forms of heathenism, or amid the refinement of art and culture, or even under the guise of a nominal Christianity – everywhere the world lieth in darkness, and is in its principles and aims the very opposite of the kingdom of God and of heaven. The pursuit of the visible, the assertion of man's will against that of God, the pride of man's wisdom are its distinguishing characteristics, in contrast with the will and the love and the service of the invisible God.

Jesus Christ came to deliver us out of this present evil world, by freeing us from its spirit, and making us partakers of the life and the powers of the heavenly world. In his conversations with the rulers of this world, both among the Jews and before Pilate, he more than once gave expression to the truth: 'Ye are of this world, I am from above; I am not of this world', and 'my kingdom is not of this world'. This other worldliness he claimed for his disciples too: 'They are not of the world, even as I am not of the world.' 'Because ye are not of the world ... therefore the world hateth you.' He described his work as an overcoming of the world and a casting out of the prince of the world. He encouraged his disciples to expect and endure the enmity of the world in the power of his victory. The life he brought with him from heaven, and came to impart to us, was one as different from that of the world, yes, more so than heaven is higher than earth. The great object of his work was to deliver us from this present evil world, according to the will of God.

This is an aspect of truth that enters into the all too little preaching or practise of our days. We sometimes hear of a worldly Christianity, and of a religious world, but there appears to be but little conception of the extent to which a worldly spirit pervades and enfeebles the Christian life. We are all of us so born and bred under the power of the spirit of the world, we are so little warned of the need of our entire deliverance from that spirit by the Spirit of God deepening it and taking its place, it is so difficult exactly to define or recognise its spirit and influence, that one often sees an earnest and active religious life with but little of the truly unworldly and heavenly spirit. As a consequence of this, the power of Jesus Christ, and of faith in him, overcoming the world, and proving that we are just as little of the world as he was, is little sought or known. Our Lord gave himself that he might deliver us from this present evil world according to the will of God: is it any wonder that his full revelation in the heart is so little enjoyed? Only he who seeks to have Jesus do his perfect work, and is ready for complete separation and emancipation from the spirit of the world, can expect it.

Let each one of us who would prove, who would know and do, the perfect will of God, study the lesson: God wills complete deliverance from this present evil world. To this end Jesus Christ gave himself for us: as we receive him to live in us, that will will be done in us. We are surrounded on every side by the powers of which the spirit of this world has possession, and are unable to resist, or even to recognise them, unless they are revealed to us by the Spirit of God. In the literature and the newspaper press of the day, in all the interest and attraction of politics and commerce, of culture and pleasure, we are carried along without knowing it. In our own hearts, the love of self with its honour and pleasure, the desire of and dependence on the visible, the lack of absolute surrender to God and his will, are all so many tokens of the worldly spirit. Not until we allow the Spirit of God to convict us of all this, and to possess us with all that is its opposite, can we fully know what the deliverance is that Christ gives according to the will of God.

May God help us to connect inseparably the three blessed truths set before us here: the will of God as the source, Jesus giving himself for us as the means of deliverance from this present evil world, as the mark and fruit of the great salvation. May he teach that we are just as little of this world as Jesus was, because we are one with him. And may the presence and power of the Son of God from heaven in our hearts, with its complete

deliverance from a worldly spirit, be known as in very
deed the will of God for us.

Chapter 19

Filled with the Knowledge of God's Will

> *'We ... do not cease to pray for you ... that ye might be filled with the knowledge of his will in all wisdom and spiritual understanding.'*
> Colossians 1:9

To understand the place of this prayer in the Christian life, and to realise how being filled with the knowledge of God's will in all spiritual wisdom lies at the very root of its growth and health, just notice what a beautiful description of the walk of a believer follows on this prayer, as the blessing it is meant to bring. The result of being filled with the knowledge of God's will will be, that we 'walk worthy of the Lord unto all pleasing, being fruitful in every good work, and increasing in the knowledge of God; Strengthened with all might, according to his glorious power, unto all patience and longsuffering with joyfulness; Giving thanks unto the Father.' Walking worthily of God and pleasing him; being fruitful; increasing in the knowledge of God; being strengthened with all might; all patience and longsuffering with joy and thanksgiving – such is the sure portion of a soul 'filled with the knowledge of his will in all wisdom and spiritual understanding.' It is the will of God that all these things should be in us and abound. Where the heart is filled with the knowledge of the will, the life will be filled with its fruits.

We have before spoken of the knowledge of God's will. The great truth suggested by these words in regard to it is, that it must be in 'all wisdom and spiritual understanding.' There is a wisdom and an understanding of the truths of Scripture which is not spiritual. The human mind can study and apprehend the doctrines which the Bible teaches concerning God and the divine life in man, without having any true apprehension of them in their quickening life and power. Christians, to a very large extent, study their Bible, listen to preaching, read religious books, in the confidence that they are earnestly desirous of knowing the truth, and able to some extent to grasp it, while the real spiritual wisdom and understanding to make it their own, to prove its power in their life, is not waited for from God. They wonder why so much Bible knowledge does not make them humble and lowly as they would like to be. They never know that it is simply because their knowledge of God's will is in the power of human wisdom and the natural understanding. And such knowledge is powerless to work effectually what God's Word is promised to work.

In his farewell discourse our Lord said to his disciples, 'the Holy Ghost ... shall teach you all things, and bring all things to your remembrance, whatsoever I have said unto you.' 'The Spirit of truth ... will guide you into all truth.' To the Holy Spirit alone was thus committed the power of teaching divine truth, and leading men into it. He was to teach all things, to guide into all truth; no truth could be known truly without his teaching. As the indwelling Spirit, possessing and renewing the heart, he alone could so impart the truth, that it becomes part of our very nature, giving both the will and the power to obey it. Our Lord had taught his disciples many things while on earth with them. But how little had they understood? Still less were they able to obey his commands of self denial, and meekness, and humility, and love. With the Holy Spirit coming down from heaven into their hearts as the power of God, and as the Spirit of his Son, the words of God would come to them in their spiritual, supernatural, quickening power.

We need to study this. As no one can worship God in spirit and in truth but through the Holy Spirit, so, no one, not even a true Christian, can have any spiritual understanding of God's will, but by the Holy Spirit. The one reason that our knowledge of God's will is so defective in its extent and power, that we see so little beauty in God's will, and we so little delight or ever succeed in fulfilling it, is simply this: the knowledge is not 'in all wisdom and spiritual understanding.'

And what is needed to get this spiritual wisdom through the Holy Spirit's teaching? One great thing – we must be spiritual people. Paul says to the Corinthians, 'I could not speak unto you as unto spiritual, but as unto carnal.' They were unfit for full spiritual teaching, because they were not spiritually minded. This suggests to us the law of all the Holy Spirit's teaching. We cannot communicate spiritual truths to those whose lives are worldly, selfish, carnal. He asks a disposition that, at least, longs to be spiritual. It is in the heart he gives his teaching. The man who yields his life to be led and ruled by him, will be taught by him. Such a one can be filled with the knowledge of God's will.

Mark the word 'filled'. It points to an emptying out and putting aside of all else. It suggests a heart given up wholly and entirely to the will of God. It promises a life in which the will of God shall spontaneously enter the minutest details of daily life – the whole heart filled with it. It is not the thought of a multitude of commandments all strung together, but of God's grand will, as the controlling power of the life, inspiring and animating the whole being. The two thoughts accompany and are the complement of each other – the whole being surrendered to be spiritual and receive spiritual wisdom, and the whole being thus filled with the knowledge of God's will.

For this Paul did not cease to pray and make request for the Colossians. Let us pray for God's church and ourselves, that the spiritual filling with the knowledge of God's will may be given us. The blessing is waiting for us. The Father delights to give it. It is our birthright – a divine birth needs and has the promise of a divine education. The Spirit through whom we received the divine life can alone, will most surely, guide us unto all its riches. Let us pray unceasingly, honestly, believingly to be – 'filled with the knowledge of his will in all wisdom and spiritual understanding.'

In heaven the will of God is done. Nothing but the heavenly life can do it. None but God's Spirit can do God's will. Let us not expect to know or do it without the heavenly life working in us by the Spirit come from heaven into our heart. The heavenly life delights in God's will. This is one of the great lessons that the church needs to learn, that the almost universal complaint of lack of power to perform, has but one cause, the heavenly life in the power of the Holy Spirit is so little known or sought.

Christian friend, learn well the lesson, that no knowledge and no book can profit you except as it reminds you of the need of the one only Teacher, the Spirit of truth, and leads you in inward adoration and teachableness to wait for the hidden spiritual wisdom which he gives in the inward part.

Chapter 20

Standing Perfect in All the Will of God

> *'Epaphras, who is one of you, a servant of Christ, saluteth you, always labouring fervently for you in prayers, that ye may stand perfect and complete in all the will of God.'*
> Colossians 4:12

In the first chapter of the epistle we had Paul praying, here we have Epaphras. The prayers of both had reference to this one thing – of such supreme consequence is it in the Christian life – the will of God. Paul prayed that their hearts might be filled with the spiritual knowledge of God's will, then they would walk worthy of the Lord to all pleasing. Epaphras prays that their lives may be so filled with that will, that they may stand complete in all the will of God. Paul says that he does not cease to pray thus. Of Epaphras he says that he always strives for them in his prayers. In both cases the relation to God's will is to be no partial or divided one – but whole and entire as expressed by the word 'all'. Paul asks that they may be filled with the knowledge of his will in all spiritual wisdom, to walk worthy of the Lord unto all pleasing. Epaphras strives for them in his prayers that they may stand complete in all the will of God. Nothing less than all God's will is to be the standard, the desire, the prayer, the hope of the believer.

To stand perfect in all the will of God – the believer's only standard. How can it be otherwise? The will of God is one whole, all equally divine, and beautiful, and blessed. All, all of equal obligation, equally needful for our peace and perfection, with equal provision made for its performance in the grace that is in Christ Jesus. The will of God is so entirely one with the nature, the perfection and the love of God, that to neglect or refuse any part of it is making it impossible for God fully to reveal himself to us and bless us. As perfect and complete as the will of God is as a whole, ought to be the believer's acceptance of and surrender to it as his only standard.

Paul and Epaphras regarded this as an attainable measure of perfection among the Colossians. There are many Christians who admit that the words express the Scripture standard of duty, but rob that admission of all its power by counting it impossible. The standard is only an ideal one, not really practicable or practical. They regard it very much as the law of Moses, with its demands that never can be fulfilled. They do not understand the words 'Ye are not under law', which demands what you cannot do, and gives no power to do, 'but under grace', which demands only what it will give and work in you, and so enables you to do all its demands. All his will is God's standard for us, actually asked and provided for; let it be ours too. Your Father asks nothing less; let nothing less be what you ask of him and offer him.

To stand complete in all the will of God – the believer's one desire. Desire is the one great power in

the world that urges and enables men to undertake and
accomplish what at first sight appears impossible. When
a man has set his heart upon a thing, difficulties only
rouse his energy and increase his power. Oh that Christians might be taught and trained to set their heart upon
'all the will of God' as their highest and only blessedness,
upon 'standing perfect in it' as the one hope of their calling. It is to be feared that the preaching of the will of
God has not had the same place as the preaching of the
grace of God. Men have not seen that as the grace is
nothing but the will of God manifested, and as it came
through Christ doing that will, so its one object is to
unite us with that will, and have it done in us as it is done
in heaven. Doing the will of God has been something
additional, a supplement to what the grace of God has
done, an expression of gratitude, instead of being the
very love, and salvation, and blessedness out of which
the grace came and into which it leads. If we understood
this, how every desire for help from God for salvation,
and happiness, and the enjoyment of his love, would be
identified with a standing complete in all that will in
which God is revealed and is alone to be found. Let us
set our heart upon it.

To stand perfect in all the will of God – the believer's
continual prayer. The teaching about the knowledge of
God's will, and the standing complete in God's will,
comes in telling of Paul's unceasing prayer and Epaphras' striving always. It is not earnest thought, or clear
apprehension, or strong desire, that will bring us what
we need – but unceasing prayer. Doing the will of God is
the life of heaven, because God is there, and works his
will without hindrance in all the holy spirits who are
wholly yielded up to him and wait upon him. It is from
God in heaven that this heavenly life of doing his will
must come down. And it will come down and be carried
on and maintained in us just in proportion as we too wait
upon God, yield ourselves to him, and continue offered
up to his Holy Spirit to work in us. Whether it be in the
quiet, steady perseverance of our daily prayer, or in the

fervent striving in seasons when the need and the desire
are specially felt, or in the inward supplication of the
heart that prays without ceasing – it is only the life that
is continually looking upward, and depending alone
upon God's working his own will in us, that will feel that
God's standard is not too high, because what the word of
his mouth demands, the power of his hand performs.

To stand complete in all the will of God – the
believer's sure hope. Paul and Epaphras were praying
out of their blessed experience. We, alas, have grown so
accustomed to use words in prayer for things we never
expect. They lived so under the power of the Holy Spirit;
they saw, notwithstanding so much to grieve and disap-
point them, some whom they could call spiritual men;
that they knew that in answer to their prayer it would be
given – men 'filled with the knowledge of his will in all
wisdom and spiritual understanding,' men 'standing
complete in all the will of God.' Let us pray without ceasing, let us strive always, for the churches or the saints
with whom we are connected, that these two prayers
may be fulfilled in them. Let us to that end ask God to
reveal in ourselves and our experience their full truth
and meaning. Amid all disappointment let us say: 'My
soul, hope thou in God! I shall yet praise him for the help
of his countenance! Let us set our hope upon God, who
worketh all things after the purpose of his will.' 'God
must ever be God alone. Heaven and the heavenly
nature are his, and must for ever be received only from
him, and for ever be only preserved by an entire trust in
him.' God alone can work his will in us. In a heart that
prays and waits without ceasing in dependence upon
him, he can and will do it. Let us believe that these precious words of Epaphras' prayer are not vain; in them
the Holy Spirit reveals the sure hope of every believer
who will trust God. Let us not doubt, but 'stand perfect
and complete in all the will of God.'

Chapter 21

The Will of God Your Sanctification

'For this is the will of God, even your sanctification.' 1 Thessalonians 4:3

The apostle had closed the third chapter of this epistle with the wondrous prayer for the Thessalonian believers, that the Lord might 'establish their hearts unblameable in holiness before our God and Father.' He proceeds in chapter 4 to urge them to walk well-pleasing to God. He begins by specially warning against two sins, uncleanness and fraud (4:3–7). And then just as he had pleaded with God to establish them unblameable in holiness, so he pleads with them to remember and yield to the blessed truth: 'This is the will of God, your sanctification.' 'God hath not called us unto uncleanness, but unto holiness.' The great plea against sin is that we are called to be holy. And the great power for holiness is the knowledge that it is God's will for us.

And what is holiness? God alone is the holy one. There is none holy but the Lord. There is no holiness but his. And nothing can be holy except as he makes it holy. 'Be ye holy for I am holy. I am the Lord which sanctify you.' Holiness is the very nature of God, inseparable from his being, and can only be communicated by his communicating himself and his own life. We are in Christ, who is made of God unto us sanctification. The Spirit of God is the Spirit of holiness. We are God's elect in sanctification of the Spirit, 'chosen to salvation through sanctification of the Spirit.' The three-in-one God is the thrice holy one, and Father, Son and Spirit each share to make us holy. The first step in sanctification is our recognising how God makes us holy. We have been sanctified in Christ Jesus. The new nature we have derived from him has been created in true holiness. Our part is in the power of the new, divine, holy nature, to act out its impulses and principles. Our justification and our sanctification are equally in Christ, by union with him, and therefore equally of faith. It is as we believe in God through Christ and the Spirit, working in us, that the inflow of the holy life from above is renewed, and that we have the courage and the power to live out the precepts that reveal the way in which that life is to act. Like the whole of salvation, sanctification, or the life of holiness, is the result of man's co-operating with God. That means first of all his entire dependence on and surrender to the divine operation, as the only source of goodness or strength. And then the acting out in life and conduct all that God has worked within us.

And what is now the help we can get from the words, 'This is the will of God, your sanctification?' The first thought is that of the divine obligation of holiness. God wills it. It is not enough to regard it in the other aspects in which it can be presented. It is indeed an essential element of the Christian life, the great proof of our gratitude for our deliverance from the guilt of sin, indispensable to true peace and happiness, our only preparation for heaven. All this is of great importance. But behind all this there is something of still greater force. We need to realise that God wills it. In eternity God predestinated us to be holy; we are 'elect according to the foreknowledge of God in sanctification of the Spirit' (Eph 1:4; 1 Pet 1:2). God's whole purpose, as a holy God, was to make us holy as he is holy. The whole of redemption was ordered with a view to this. It is not only one of his commands, among many; it is the command which includes all. The whole being and character of God proclaim it; the whole nature and aim of redemption call for it. Believers, God wills your sanctification. Worship God in his holiness, until every thought of God in his glory and grace is connected with the deep conviction: This blessed God wills my holiness. Rest not until your will has surrendered unconditionally to the will of God, and found its true destiny in receiving that divine will and working it out.

A second thought that suggests itself is that of the divine possibility of holiness. We have learnt in our meditations that the will of God is not only a divine purpose of what is to do, or a divine precept as to what we are to do, but a divine energy that works out its own purpose. All that God wills he works. Not indeed in those who refuse to accept or submit to that will. They have the power to resist it. But in those who yield their consent, who love that will and long that it should be done on earth as in heaven, God himself worketh out all things after the purpose of his will. In every man with a sound strong will, it seeks at once to embody itself in action, and to effect what has been regarded an object of desire. God works in us both to will and to do. When he has worked the will, he delights, if he be waited on and yielded to, to work the doing. When, by his grace, the believer wills as God wills, when he has accepted God's will for sanctification as his own will, he can count upon God's working it. God wills it with all the energy of his divine being. God can as little cease working holiness as he can cease being holy or being God. He wills our sanctification. And if we will but will it too, in the faith of the new nature in which the Holy Spirit works, and yield ourselves to the will of omnipotent love, in the assurance of his working in us, we shall experience how true and blessed the message is: God wills and therefore most certainly works your sanctification.

The third lesson suggested by our text is – the divine means of holiness. The will of God is your sanctification – that is, all that God wills has this one object. Whether it be his will in the eternal counsel, or here in time in providence, whether in mercy or in judgment, whether in precept or promise, all that God wills concerning us is our sanctification. This gives a new meaning, and is our true glory, to every command of Scripture. The commands of God have unspeakable value as marking out for us that path of safety and of life, as guiding us to all that is lovely and of good report. But here is their highest glory: through them the holy one seeks to make us partakers of his own holiness. Do let us learn to regard every indication of God's will, in Scripture or in nature, in things great or little, as the will of the holy one, coming to make us holy. Let every thought of God's will fill us with the longing and the hope to be holy. And let every thought of holiness lead us to the study of, and the delight in, and the faithful doing of God's will. Let every sin that God's Word forbids, such as those Paul mentions, uncleanness and fraud, be put far from us. Let everything that is of the earthly, carnal, selfish nature be put off, that the whole spirit, soul and body may be sanctified: let every command that points to the true Christlike life, humility, and love, and self-sacrifice, be welcomed as the channel of God's holiness. The desire after and delight and faith in God's holiness and God's will will become inseparably one.

Let all who would experience this remember one thing. It is because it is God's will and God's holiness that there is power and life and blessing in it. Everything depends upon our knowing God and waiting on him, coming under the operation of his holy presence and power. As we know him as the living God, and have communion with him as the holy, living, almighty, ever-present and ever-working One, his will and his holiness will become to us heavenly realities, and we shall know how certainly, how blessedly, his will is actually our sanctification.

Chapter 22

Unceasing Thanksgiving, the Will of God

> '*In everything give thanks: for this is the will of God in Christ Jesus concerning you.*'
> 1 Thessalonians 5:18

'In everything give thanks' – that means a life of unceasing joy. The bestowment of a gift makes me glad. Giving thanks is the expression of that gladness to the giver. For what in the gift he has bestowed, for what he has proved himself to be as a friend, my happiness offers him all it has to give, all he desires – the acknowledgement of indebtedness and obligation and grateful love. Every father does his utmost to make his children happy; he loves not only to see them happy, but to see them connect their happiness with himself and his love. It is the will of God that in everything, in every circumstance and condition, the whole life of his child should be one of unceasing praise and thanksgiving. If it be not always so with us, let us set ourselves to learn the lesson: In everything give thanks: for this is the will of God in Christ Jesus concerning you.

In everything give thanks: there is good reason for it. God is not a hard master, who reaps where he has not sown. He never commands joy without giving abundant cause for it. He does not expect thanks where there is nothing to thank for. He would have us remember that, in the most trying circumstances and the deepest sorrow, there is cause for thanksgiving infinitely outweighing any reason for mourning. Whatever we lose, God and his love are still left us. The very loss is meant to make the love more precious: the trial is love seeking to give itself more completely to us. Whatever we lose, there is always the unspeakable gift – God's own Son to be our portion and our friend. Whatever we lose, there is always a peace that passeth understanding, a joy that is unspeakable, a riches of glory that will supply every need, an abounding grace that perfects Christ's strength in our weakness. There are always the exceeding great and precious promises, and the heavenly treasures that cannot pass away. God is educating us through loss and trial, into the full enjoyment of our heavenly heritage and the perfect fitness for his own fellowship. So let us believe that the command is most reasonable, and say that this will of God, in everything give thanks, is ours too.

In everything give thanks – this is both the mark and the means of a vigorous Christian life. It draws us off from ourselves, and fixes the heart upon God. It lifts us above the world, and makes us more than conquerors through him who loved us. It places our peace, our happiness, our life, beyond the reach of circumstances. So far from rendering us indifferent to the suffering of our fellowmen, it fills us with hope in seeking to relieve them, it teaches us what joy there is in the kindness and love of God, and makes that the keynote of our life. It gives wings to our prayer, our faith, our love, to live the true heavenly life in God's presence and worship. It ennobles in torment every temptation with the hallelujah of victory.

In everything give thanks. God himself will work it in you. This is the will of God in Christ Jesus concerning you. We have seen more than once that the will of God is a loving, almighty power, working out its own purpose with our intelligent consent. We are co-workers with God – that means, not that he does part and we do part, but that he does all in us and we do all through him. It means that he works in us to will and to do, and that we, through faith in his working, in the power that worketh in us, work out his will. Just because it is the will of God, the believing soul is sure that it can be. It is the will of God in Christ. The expression is so frequent that its meaning is passed over. All that God is and does to us, he is and does through our Lord Jesus. The Father does nothing in us but through the Son. The Son does nothing but as the Father does it through him. Our experience of God's work in us depends upon our abiding in Christ, our drawing and remaining near to God in and through Christ. To a soul seeking its life in Christ alone, the will of God ensures a life of unceasing praise and thanks.

In everything give thanks – it needs a life of entire consecration. Many of God's commands become an unbearable burden, an impossible strain, because we look to the feeble, sickly life to do what only the strength of vigorous health can perform. We cannot take up one part of God's will, and do it when we please. A life of undivided and absolute surrender to all God's will is the condition of being able to perform any part of it effectively. Every command to perform some special part of God's will is a call to enquire whether we have accepted all his will as the law of our life. The soul that has done this, that is learning the lesson of daily guidance for daily duty, and is prepared to meet every new demand, with the question as to its implicit submission to that will, and its unquestioning confidence in the provision of sufficient strength, all settled, has found the secret of obedience to this command too. When God is known as our exceeding joy, when a walk in the light of his countenance all the day is counted equally a privilege and an indispensable necessity, the giving of thanks in everything is not looked upon as a hopeless attainment. Because it is the will of a loving and almighty Father, that will can be done.

In everything give thanks! These are indeed the Christians the world stands in need of. It is the happy Christian – not the happy man who happens also to be a Christian, but – the Christian who proves that happiness is in God, and who lives the life of joy and praise because he lives in God's presence, who will find the joy of the Lord his strength in God's service, and who will be the best witness to what the grace of God can do to give true joy and blessing. It is the will of God in Christ to us. Let us rest content with nothing less.

Chapter 23

The Salvation of All the Will of God

'I exhort therefore, that, first of all, supplications, prayers, intercessions, and giving of thanks, be made for all men ... this is good and acceptable in the sight of God our Saviour; Who will have all men to be saved.'
1 Timothy 2:1–4

'The Lord is ... longsuffering to us-ward, not willing that any should perish, but that all should come to repentance.' 2 Peter 3:9

After Paul had urged that supplications, prayers and intercessions should be made for all men, he reminds us that we may do so in confident assurance that it is good and acceptable to God, because he willeth that all men should be saved. The knowledge and faith of his will for all is to be the motive and the measure of our prayer for all. What God in heaven wills and works for his children on earth we are to will and work for too. As we enter into his will for all, we shall know what we are to do to fulfil that will. And as we pray and labour for all, the faith in his will for all will inspire us with confidence and love.

Perhaps the question arises, – If God wills the salvation of all, how is it that it is not effected? What of the doctrine of election, as Scripture teaches it us? And what of the omnipotence of God, which is surely equal to the love that wills the salvation of all? As to election, let us remember that there are mysteries in God and in Scripture which are beyond our reach. If there are apparently conflicting truths which we cannot reconcile, we know that Scripture was not written, like a book of science, to satisfy the intellect, but as the revelation of the hidden wisdom of God, to test and strengthen faith and submission, to waken love and childlike teachableness. If we cannot understand why his power does not work what his will has purposed, we shall find that, as the creation of man with a free will is an act by which the will of God has limited itself, all that God does or does not do is decided by conditions far beyond our understanding, and which it needs a divine wisdom to grasp and to order. We shall learn that God's will is as much beyond our comprehension as God's being, and that it is our wisdom and safety and happiness to accept every revealed truth with the simplicity and the faith of little children, and yield ourselves to it to prove its living power within our hearts. Let us not fear to yield ourselves to the uttermost of this blessed word: 'God willeth that all men should be saved.'

God is love. His will is love. As he makes his sun to shine on the good and the evil, so his love rests upon all. However little we can understand why his love is longsuffering and patient, and does not take its power and reign, we believe and know the love that God has to us – a love whose measure in heaven is the gift of his Son, and on earth every child of man. His love is nothing but his will in its divine energy doing its very utmost, in accordance with the divine law by which his relation to his creature is regulated, to make men partakers of its blessedness. His will is nothing but his love in its infinite patience and tenderness delighting to win and bless every heart into which it can gain access. If we only knew God and his love, how we should look upon every man we see as one upon whom that love rests and for whom it longs. We should begin to wonder at the mystery of grace that has taken up the church, as the body of Christ, as a partner in the great work of making that love known, and has rendered itself dependent upon its faithfulness. And we should see that all living to do God's will must lead up to this as its central glory: our doing the will that wills that all should be saved.

'God willeth that all men should be saved.' This truth is a supernatural mystery, not to be apprehended but by a spiritual mind through the teaching of the Holy Spirit. It is in itself so divine and beyond our apprehension, the difficulties that surround it are so many and so real, it needs so much of time, and of the sacrifice of the humble loving heart, to master its teaching, that to very many the words carry but little meaning. To the believer who in very deed seeks to know and do all God's will they give a new meaning to life. He begins to see that his call to love and to save his fellowmen is not something accidental or additional that, along with other things, goes up to make his life, and to which he can devote as much of time and thought as he sees fit. He learns that just as this loving, saving will of God is the secret source of all his will, rules it all, so this loving, saving will is to be the chief thing he lives for too. I have been redeemed and organically united to and made a member of the saving Christ, who came to do this will of the Father. I have been chosen and set apart and fitted for this as the one object of my being in the world. I begin to see faintly that the prayer, 'Thy will be done!' means above everything that I give myself for this loving, saving will of God to possess, to inspire, to use, if need be to consume me.

And I feel the need of spelling out the words of the sentence till my heart can call them its own: God – my God, who liveth in me – willeth, with his whole heart, in that will which he has revealed to his people that they may carry it into effect – that all men, here around me, and to the ends of the earth – should be saved, should have everlasting life.

Paul wrote these words in connection with a call to prayer for all men. Our faith in the truth of God's loving, saving will must be put into practice. It must stir us to prayer. And prayer will most certainly stir us to work. We must not only seek to believe and feel the truth of these words, but must act. This will of God must be done. Let us look upon those around us as the objects of God's love, whom his saving will is seeking to reach. Let us, as we yield ourselves to this will go and speak to those around of God's love in Christ. It is possible that we are not succeeding in doing God's will in our personal life because we neglect this chief thing. As we pray to be possessed and filled with the knowledge of this will of God, let us, in our Sunday School class, or gospel work, in our efforts for young and old, for poor and rich, seek to have hearts filled with this love, tongues that speak of Jesus and his salvation, and a will that finds its strength in God's own will – that all men should be saved. So will our life, and our love, and our work, and our will in some measure be like that of Jesus Christ – a doing of the Father's will.

Chapter 24

Lo, I Come to Do Thy Will

'Then said I, Lo, I come to do thy will, O God ... By the which will we are sanctified through the offering of the body of Jesus Christ once for all.' Hebrews 10:7–10

'Lo, I come ... I delight to do thy will, O my God.' Psalm 40:7–8

David had said: 'Sacrifices and offerings thou wouldest not, neither hadst pleasure therein.' They had been appointed for a time, as a shadow or picture; they were not what God sought or could please him; they were not really the will of God. David understood that what God wanted was the doing of his will, and said: 'I delight to do thy will, O my God.' While saying this of himself, he spoke it of Christ, in whom alone its true fulfilment could be found. These are the great words with which Christ coming into the world announces his work: 'Lo, I am come to do thy will, O God.' If we are really to penetrate to the very heart of what Christ is, and means, of what he did for us and does in us, we must seek to know him as come from heaven to earth to do the will of God, and so to restore the doing of God's will on earth to the place it has in heaven.

His doing of God's will is first contrasted with the sacrifices and offerings of the Old Testament worship, and then specially connected with the offering of his own body once for all. Of this will of God, as thus done by him, even unto death, we are taught that in it we have been sanctified, because by one offering he hath perfected for ever them that are sanctified. Let us try and learn the great lessons that there are to be found here in connection with our study of the will of God.

The doing of God's will is the only worship that is pleasing to God. It was this alone that gave their value to the Old Testament sacrifices. Not in the costliness or the multitude of the offerings lay their value, but in the disposition, the contrition, or the faith, or the consecration of which they were the expression. Not even in these however, except as they were a divine appointment, and were brought in accordance with God's own command. If not accompanied by obedience they were worse than useless. 'Obedience is better than sacrifice.' 'Thou desirest not sacrifice ... Thou delightest not in burnt-offering ... the sacrifices of God are ... a broken heart.' It is as far as they were the doing of God's will that they were well-pleasing. And so they became the symbols of a life given up in devotion to God, wholly yielded to his will and service. The doing of God's will was the secret of acceptable worship.

Christ came to this world to do the will of God. He came and lived as man to show us that the one thing God asks of the creature, that the one thing that can bring the creature life and blessedness, is the doing of the will of God. With this view he not only submitted himself to all the commandments and ordinances of the law; in all his life and work, in his eating and speaking, in his travels and miracles, he lived a life of absolute dependence upon God's guidance – in everything he did only God's will, he did all God's will. He knew that it was God's will that He should die as a propitiation for our sins. As the time came near, and all that would imply opened up before his human nature, he had more than once occasion to say: 'How am I straitened! Now it is my soul troubled! My soul is sorrowful even unto death!' But through it all he thought of God's will; the surrender to God's will sustained him. And he gave himself to be what the sin-offering and burnt-offering had only typified, a sacrifice unto God, obedient even unto death. This gave his inconceivable suffering its inconceivable value, it was borne as the will of God laying God's just judgment upon him that the guilty might go free.

It is Christ's doing the will of God even unto death that has effected our salvation. 'By the which will we are sanctified through the offering of the body of Jesus Christ once for all.' The word sanctified is used here in its larger sense, as it includes justification and regeneration, and the whole of redemption; restored to the fellowship of God, and taken possession of by him. The great sin of Adam and of mankind was doing their own will instead of God's will. The great, the only root of all sin and misery was self-will. Jesus Christ came to take away sin. He did so by a life and a death of the most perfect sacrifice of his will to the will of God. He bore the consequence, the punishment, the curse that our self-will had brought. Through his perfect obedience to God's will he made a perfect atonement for our sin, and won for the will of God its place of supremacy in this sinful world. He did this by the offering of his body, once for all, and so has perfected for ever them that are sanctified. 'By the obedience of one, many are made righteous.' As the partakers of a complete and perfect righteousness, won by obedience to the will of God, as 'created after the image of God in righteousness', their entrance into the perfect love and life of God is complete and for ever.

The doing to God's will by which Christ won our salvation is now and ever the power of the salvation he imparts. Doing God's will is not only, as many think, the price by which salvation was won. It is salvation itself. In Christ doing God's will was the power that conquered every temptation to self-will, that proved what human life ought really to be, that brought a perfect human life and laid it as a sacrifice at God's feet, that broke for ever the power of self-will in its dominion over us. In Christ it proved that sacrificing self-will to the very utmost, doing the will of God even unto death, is the path to the fullness of the life and glory of God. In Christ, doing the will of God is seen to be the life and joy of heaven brought down to earth, and the power to rise from earth to heaven. Doing God's will is at once the cause, the object, the power, the blessedness of salvation.

It is only by Christ in us that we can in any measure do the will of God on earth as it is done in heaven. The prayer that Christ taught us was meant to be heard; God answers it in many various degrees. To pray it daily means to aim at it in the power of God's answer. And yet how many earnest Christians who are utterly hopeless in regard to it. Their surrender to do God's will is ever failing. It is not the great reason that they are attempting it in the power of a life that is not wholly possessed by Jesus Christ? Listen to his word: 'Lo, I am come to do thy will.' All power to do God's will is in him. As we can truly say, Christ liveth in me, his strength is perfected in our weakness. The call comes to each believer, as one sanctified in the will of God, by the offering of the body of Jesus Christ once for all, and perfected for evermore, to accept the will of God as done by Christ for us, as still being done in us by him, as God's free gift in Christ Jesus. The only thing needed, when the heart sees and accepts and loves and vows this doing of God's will as its one desire, is the faith that Jesus does take charge of a surrendered will, and that in the power of him who lives in heaven and lives in us, the doing of God's will can become our daily life.

Chapter 25

Doing the Will of God Obtains the Promise

'Ye have need of patience, that, after ye have done the will of God, ye might receive the promise.' Hebrews 10:36

It was in a time of very severe trial that this epistle was addressed to the Hebrews. It had been to them a bitter disappointment to see the nation rejecting their messiah. To have the temple, too, with its divine ordinances of circumcision and sacrifice, set aside, was to many a mystery and a cause of deep sorrow. In reproach and the spoiling of their goods they had had personally to endure the pain of persecution. The epistle was written to comfort them by revealing the spiritual glory of Christ's priesthood and the salvation he wanted. And it pointed them to the Father, to prove that suffering had been the path of all God's saints, and had always brought a great recompense of reward. It is in this connection that the words come: 'Ye have need of patience, that, after ye have done the will of God, ye might receive the promise.' The promise was sure, and very precious; the suffering was needful, and would be very blessed. The one thing they needed was patience in bearing what God sent, and waiting for what God had promised. And in that time of patient waiting they needed just one thing – to see that they did the will of God. In a world of sorrow and trial the Christian has but one thing to strive after: not only to bear, but to do the will of God; that, having done the will of God, you might receive the promise.

Doing the will of God is the path to the inheritance. God's will working in us can alone fit us for receiving and enjoying it. And God's will can work in no other way in us as creatures endowed with intelligence and will and moral powers, than by our doing it. Not in any way as a matter of work or merit, but in the very nature and necessity of things the only way of our receiving the promise, which has been bestowed of grace, is by our doing the will. We have been looking at the will of God in various aspects – let us once again turn to this, one of the most elementary, and yet one of the deepest, truths connected with it.

'After ye have done the will of God.' It has been said the highest form of existence is the power of working. It is so in God. All his attributes could not make him the glorious God he is, if they were all dormant, inactive powers. His love, for instance, would be a mere thought or sentiment, not in deed and truth. The highest form of human existence is even so the power of working; and, as a creature, the highest form of that power can be nothing than working out the perfect will of God. God works to will and to do in us, what he works in us we work out, doing what he wills and does in us. Such doing of the will of God is the proof of our entire surrender to it, our being truly mastered and possessed by it. Such doing the will of God is what gives its strength to our inner man, refines and spiritualises our whole being, and fits us for being here, the abode of the three-in-one God (John 14:15,21,23), and entering his abode hereafter (Matt 7:21). Such doing the will of God fits a Christian for receiving every promise.

It was in the time of suffering and trial that these believers were thus to do the will of God. The first concern of most Christians in trouble is to be delivered from it. This may not be the chief thing. The one great desire ought to be – in nothing to fail of knowing or doing the will of God. This is the secret of strength and true nobility in the Christian life. Some think that if under reproach or persecution or injustice, evil feelings are roused and given way to, there is some excuse for it – it cannot be judged too severely – the temptation was so great. God's Word teaches us differently. It regards the Christian so entirely as a man who has given up his own will to live wholly for God's will, that it says to him, of all trial and temptation of whatever nature, seek one thing: not to sin against God. Be patient, and see that you do the will of God.

But is not this something beyond human power – in every trial to think first of God's will, and do that? It is indeed something beyond human power, but not beyond the power of grace. It is just for this that our Lord Jesus came to earth, saying: 'I come to do thy will, O God!' and went to the cross with the cry: 'Not my will, but thine, be done.' He lived to give us an example of how we ought to live. He died to set us free from the power of sin, and open the path, through death to sin and self, to a life for God and his will. He ascended to heaven to give his own Holy Spirit, that in his power we might, like him, do the will of the Father.

Alas, that in the church of Christ the truth should be so little known that to do the will of God is the first duty of the believer; and, as a consequence of this, that there is so little desire of the promise and the need of the Holy

Spirit to teach us God's will in daily life. And still further, so little faith in the power of the grace of Christ and his Spirit to fit us for the life of doing the will of God. Men have lost sight of the supernatural light that can reveal the will of God in its beauty and attractivenesss, and make it a joy to do it; and of the supernatural obligation to live wholly and entirely for the will of that God who created us, and to whom Christ has brought us back; and of the supernatural power, corresponding to the light and the obligation, which brings a life in the will of God, within our reach, because Christ's strength is made perfect in our weakness.

Believer, whatever others say or do, take the Word in its simple divine meaning: 'Ye have need of patience, that, after ye have done the will of God, ye might receive the promise.' Beseech God, by his Holy Spirit, in the renewing of the spirit of your mind, to show you how he would have you live wholly in his will. Yield yourself to that will in everything you know, and do it. Yield yourself to that will in all its divine love and quickening power as it works in you and makes you partaker of its inmost nature. Pray, pray, pray, until you see increasingly how what Christ revealed in his life and death is the promise and pledge of what God will work in you, and how your abiding in him and your oneness with him means nothing less than your being called to do the will of God as he did it.

Chapter 26

God Himself Working His Will in Us

*'Now the God of peace ... Make you perfect
in every good work to do his will, working in
you that which is wellpleasing in his sight,
through Jesus Christ; to whom be glory for
ever and ever.'* Hebrews 13:20–21

In Hebrews we have three passages on the will of God.
The first 10:7–10, spoke of that will, and Christ's doing
it, as the cause of our redemption – the deep root in
which our life stands. The second, 10:36, spoke of that
will as done patiently by us, amid the trials of this earth.
The third, our present text, shows us the wonderful bond
of union between the two former: the same God who

wrought out that will in Christ for our redemption, is working out that will in us too. What God did in Christ is the pledge of what he will do in us too. That Christ did the will of God secures our doing that will too. Listen to the wonderful teaching.

'Now, the God of peace, who brought again from the dead the great shepherd of the sheep in the blood of the everlasting covenant, even our Lord Jesus, make you perfect to do his will.' All that is said about the Lord Jesus refers to the previous teaching of the epistle. It has taught us what the covenant was, what the blood of the covenant, what the exaltation of the throne of Christ as the priest king, the great shepherd of the sheep. And now it says that the God of peace, who did it all, who gave Christ to do his will and die on the cross, and then raised him from the dead, that the same God will perfect us to do his will. As much as it was God who sent and enabled Christ to do his will, and through that perfected him and perfected our salvation, it is God too who will perfect us in every good thing to do his will. God's will being done in us is to God of the same interest as his will done to Christ; he cares for the one as much as the other. The same omnipotence which created for Christ a body through the virgin Mary, and empowered Christ – who could do nothing of himself – to do that will, even to the agony of Gethsemane, and the surrender of his spirit into his Father's hand on Calvary, and then raised him from the grave to his own right hand, the same omnipotent God is working in you that you may do his will. Oh, for grace to believe this – the God who worked all in Christ, even to raising him from the very dead, is working all in us!

You do not catch it yet? It looks altogether too impossible. The difference is too great. The difficulties in our sinful nature are too insuperable. Come and listen once again. 'Now, the God of peace, who brought again from the dead our Lord Jesus Christ' – what now – do pause, and take in every word – 'make you perfect' – in every good work – 'to do his will.' What more could one wish?

And yet, to remove all doubt, there is more. There follows: 'working in us that which is pleasing in his sight, through Jesus Christ.' The centre words, 'to do his will', are welded fast between what precedes: 'God himself make you perfect in every good thing', and what follows – 'working himself in you that which is pleasing in his sight,' As much as God was concerned in the great redemption which Christ came to work out, he still cares for the details as they are worked out in the life of every believer. God sent and fitted Christ to do his will. He does for us nothing more and nothing less: he perfects us in every good thing to do his will.

The lessons for which we want to take these words into our heart, and which we want to ask God to teach us by the Holy Spirit, are three.

The first is: the one object of the great redemption is, to fit us to do God's will here on earth. For that we were created; that was God's image and likeness in us; that was our fitness for fellowship with God, and the participation in his rule of the word to which we were destined. To redeem and bring us back to this, God worked that stupendous miracle of power and of love; his Son becoming man, that as man he might show us how to do God's will, and how by doing it sin could be atoned and conquered. For this Christ lives in heaven and in our hearts, that through him God may work in us that which is well pleasing in his heart. What the sinner needs to know when he is called to repentance, what the believer needs to be continually reminded of and encouraged in, is this: to do God's will is what I have been redeemed for. The entire failure of so many Christian lives is due to this, that the church has not clearly and persistently preached the great message, that all God's wondrous grace has this one object, to restore us to the original glory of our creation, and make it our life, to do his will.

The second lesson is of no less importance – we can do God's will because God himself fits us for it, working in us that which is pleasing in his sight.

Alas! how little this is known or believed by believers.

The call to do all God's will is made of none effect by the terrible unbelief that says: It cannot be; I cannot do it. Men say that they believe that all the mysteries of redemption, up to Christ's resurrection and exaltation to heaven, were wrought by the 'working of his mighty power' (Eph 1:20). But they do not believe, what Scripture affirms as distinctly (Eph 1:19), that the same exceeding greatness of his power works in them that believe. Let me implore every child of God who would live to do his will, to remember: the will of God is so holy and divine; no one can do it but God himself. God has given you a renewed will, capable of knowing and desiring, and even delighting in, his will, but not of doing it in your own strength. The work of the will is to accept his will as being indeed what he will work in you. This is indeed our highest glory, that God, who, according to his very nature, must work all in all, will work in us both to will and to do. He himself fits us in every good thing to do his will, working himself in us that which is pleasing in his sight.

The last lesson follows naturally: Our great need and our great duty, when we have accepted our calling to live only to do his will, is to bow before God in continual humility and dependence, asking to know fully our utter impotence, and seeking to trust confidently in his power working in us. And with this, to understand that his power cannot work freely and fully in us, except as he dwells in us. Jesus said: 'The Father abiding in me doeth the works.' It is 'through Jesus Christ' God works in us what is pleasing in his sight. That is, through Jesus Christ dwelling in the heart, by the power of the Holy Spirit, God by a continual secret, almighty operation, works out his will in us, by fitting us to do it. The one thing needful is: a simple, but unceasing and unlimited, faith in the indwelling Jesus. 'Lo, I come', he said. 'I delight to do thy will.' That is not only for us, but in us. He is the executor of the Father's will, through whom it is all carried out. Oh, let us turn with a new consecration to do all God's will, with a new faith to God who will work in us the fitness to do it, with a new devotion to Jesus Christ, through whom we the sinful, we the impotent, can indeed have grace to say too: 'I delight to do thy will, O my God.'

Chapter 27

Suffering According to the Will of God

'For so is the will of God, that with well doing ye may put to silence the ignorance of foolish men ... if, when ye do well, and suffer for it, ye take it patiently, this is acceptable with God ... because Christ also suffered for us, leaving us an example, that ye should follow his steps.' 1 Peter 2:15,20–21

'It is better, if the will of God be so, that ye suffer for well doing, than for evil doing. For Christ also hath once suffered for sins.' 1 Peter 3:17–18

But rejoice, inasmuch as ye are partakers of Christ's sufferings ... Wherefore let them that suffer according to the will of God commit the keeping of their souls to him in well doing, as unto a faithful Creator.' 1 Peter 4:13,19

Before Peter had received the Holy Spirit, he could not understand that suffering had to be borne as God's will. When Christ spoke of his suffering he reproved him, and had to bear the rebuke: 'Get thee behind me, Satan.' When his discipleship brought him into danger and suffering, he denied his Lord. He could not see that suffering was God's will. With Pentecost everything was changed. He knew no fear. He rejoiced that he was counted worthy to suffer for his name. In his epistle he connects Christ's suffering for our sins with his example, calling us to suffer like him. Through suffering to glory is the keynote of his exhortation to the saints. Let us listen to what he teaches us of the will of God in suffering.

The first lesson is: To regard all suffering as the will of God for us. 'If the will of God be so, that ye suffer for well doing', 'them that suffer according to the will of God.' He is speaking of the suffering of injustice at the hands of our fellow-men. Very many, who think they are ready to endure trial that comes direct from God, find it very hard to bear unkind, or hard, or unjust treatment from men. And yet it is just here that Christ's teaching and example, and all scriptural instruction, call upon us to accept and bow to the will of God. Whether it be in the most flagrant injustice, and the most terrible suffering – such as our Lord endured at the hands of Caiaphas and Pilate – or the smaller vexations that we meet with in daily life from enemies or friends, all suffering must be to us the will of God. Nothing can come to us without the will of God. What is done may be most contrary to the will of God, and the doer most guilty in his sight – that it is done to us, that we suffer by it, is God's will. And the first duty of the child of God is – not to look at the man who does it, to seek to be avenged of him, or delivered from his hands, but to recognise and bow beneath it as the Father's will. That one thought – it is the Father's will – changes our feelings towards it, enables us to accept it as a blessing, changes it from an evil into a good. In all suffering let the first thought be, to see the Father's hand, and count on the Father's help. Then no circumstance whatever can for one moment take us out of the blessed will of God.

The second lesson is: Always suffer with well-doing. In all the three texts the word 'well-doing' occurs. If we suffer when we do wrong, and take it patiently, this is no glory. But if we suffer when we do well, and take it patiently, this is acceptable with God – that so by well-doing we put to silence the ignorance of foolish men. For it is better, if the will of God be so, that ye suffer for well-doing than for evil-doing. And it is in well-doing we can commit our souls unto a faithful Creator. The one thing we are to care for is that, if we suffer, it is not to be for wrong-doing, but for well-doing. And also with well-doing, not allowing the suffering to call forth anything that is sinful. That must be our one desire in suffering. It is caused by sin, it is meant to take away sin – how terrrible if I make it the occasion of more sin, and turn it to the very opposite of what God means it to be. Men may learn from us what the power of grace is, to soften and to strengthen; what the reality is of the heavenly life and the joy that enables us to bear all loss; and what the blessing is of the service of the divine Master, who can make his own path of suffering so attractive and so blessed to his followers.

Here is the third lesson: In suffering to commit our souls to God's faithful keeping. What a precious privilege! Amid all the temptation suffering brings, God himself offers to take charge of the keeping of our souls. Going down into the darkness of death, our Lord Jesus said: 'Father, into thy hands I commend my spirit.' Into every dark cloud of suffering into which we enter, we may say this too. From all the strife of tongues and the pride of man, from all that there is in ourselves of the tendency to impatience or anger, to quick judgments or unloving dispositions, the faithful Creator can keep the soul committed to him. He who sends the suffering as his will, has beforehand provided a place of safety, where the blessing of the suffering will assuredly be given. Let us say: 'I know whom I have believed, and am persuaded that he is able to keep that which I have committed unto him.'

Then comes the last lesson: In all our suffering according to the will of God, Christ is our pattern and our strength. In all the three chapters Christ's sufferings for our sake is connected with our suffering for his sake. 'Christ also suffered for us, leaving us an example – that ye should follow in his steps' (2:21). 'It is better ... that ye suffer for well doing, than for evil doing. For Christ also hath once suffered for sins, the just for the unjust' (3:17–18). 'Forasmuch as Christ hath suffered for us in the flesh, arm yourselves likewise with the same mind ... But rejoice, inasmuch as ye are partakers of Christ's sufferings ... for the spirit of glory and of God resteth upon you' (4:1,13–14). The sufferings of believers are as indispensable as are those of Christ. They are to be borne in the same spirit. They are the means of fellowship with him, and conformity to his image. Christ Jesus accepted and bore all suffering, of whatever nature, great or small, whether coming in the ordinary course of events or specially devised against himself, as the will of God. He endured it, as the necessary result of sin, in submission to the will of the Father who sent it, as the school in which he was to prove that his will was one with the Father's, and that the Father's will was over all.

Christ is our pattern, because he is our life. In time of suffering proof is given that the spirit of glory and the spirit of God rests upon us. Oh, that all believers, who desire to live wholly to the will of God, might understand how much depends upon their recognising God's will in all suffering, and bearing all according to the will of God! And might understand, too, how imposssible it is to disconnect Christ's sufferings for us from ours for him. He suffered for us as our head, in whom we are made alive. We can only suffer for him as he lives in us. The attempt to do or bear the will of God aright, as long as we are living on a different level from that on which Christ lived, must be failure. It is only where the whole-hearted surrender, to live and die for the will of God as he did, possesses the soul that the mighty power of his love and grace, and Spirit can do their wonders in the life.

Chapter 28

Living to the Will of God

'That ye no longer should live the rest of your time in the flesh to the lusts (desires) of men, but to the will of God.' 1 Peter 4:2

The believers to whom Peter writes needed to be reminded that there is a twofold possibility in the Christian life. It is possible – alas, how often it is done – even after conversion, still to live to the lusts of men, desiring and seeking what men in the world seek. It is possible, on the other hand, to turn entirely away from the living to the desires of men, and wholly live to the will of God, even as Christ had done. He had written: 'Forasmuch then as Christ hath suffered for us in the flesh, arm yourselves likewise with the same mind: for he that hath suffered in the flesh hath ceased from sin', and then continues, as the fruit of being armed with the same mind as

Christ, and having, through suffering in the flesh, been brought to cease from sin, 'live no longer to the desires of men, but to the will of God.' Every Christian stands between two contending forces. The unceasing influence of human nature and its desires, the example of the men of the world, the whole current of human society, draws him to live to the desires of men. Blessed the man who has yielded to the power of Christ and his cross, who has armed himself with the same mind, at any cost rather to suffer than to sin, and now lives even as Christ, not to the will of man, but to the will of God. Blessed the life in which the purpose of Christ's coming is being realised, and which is now wholly yielded to, wholly preserved, and controlled by the will of God.

We are approaching the close of our study of the will of God. We have had occasion to look at it from almost every possible side. The desire, the hope, the purpose, to live only to the will of God, may have been wakened or strengthened in many a heart. And yet there is the painful sense of failure, and a consciousness that there is some hidden trouble that hinders the possession of what appears so clearly promised in God's Word. Let me try to gather up all the teaching we have had, and to point out, in the simplest way possible, what appear to be the steps that lead up to the life Scripture teaches us to pray for and expect – perfect and complete in all the will of God.

1. I must mention first what often comes last in experience: To live to God's will is impossible except as to live in close and abiding fellowship with Jesus Christ. It is he who proclaimed: 'Lo, I come to do thy will, O God.' He not only had to do it alone on Calvary: the work he began there he carries on in heaven. Today, still, it is 'through Jesus Christ' alone that God works his will in us (Heb 13:21). It is impossible to bear or to do God's will as Christ did, except as we have the same mind that was in him. And we cannot have the same mind, except as we are wholly given up to him have him living in us, and seek to live in his fellowship. It is the living presence and

power of Christ in the heart that enables us to do God's will from the heart. You cannot demand of a sickly life that it shall do the work of a healthy man. It is where the sufficiency of Christ's grace is known, and our strength is made perfect in weakness, because his power rests upon us, that we can truly live to God.

2. To live to God's will demands that there be a clear and full surrender of every movement of our life to do that will. It is in the little things, in the natural, innocent things in which we do not see how God's will comes in, that failure succeeds. We need to pray very earnestly for a spiritual insight into the blessed truth, that every power, and every moment, and every movement of our life must be in harmony with that will. We are so slow to apprehend what this means, that, unless there be patient, persevering power, and a very docile waiting for the Spirit's teaching, we may struggle on for years without grasping what ought to be an elementary truth – that God's will must rule our life, as it ruled the life of Christ Jesus – that it must all be according to the will of God.

3. To live to God's will it is essential that whatever we know to be according to that will must be done at once. Very often there comes to us a subtle temptation that, until we have power to do all God's will, a small failure, additional to those which appear a necessity, is not of such consequence. Or that, as long as we have not received some special endowment of power, it is needless and vain to attempt a perfect obedience. Let us beware of giving way to such thoughts. All increase of grace and strength in a Christian's life stands under the law of faithfulness in little things. Whatever you know to be the will of God, little or great, do it at once. If you are not sure, do the nearest to what you know to be right. It is in doing what we know that we give proof of our integrity, and are prepared to receive more grace.

4. Learn also to do all your ordinary work as the will of God. There is such a vast range of ordinary everyday duty or drudgery that appears to have little direct connection with the will of God, and is consciously sepa-

rated from it. Beware of giving way to this. Study Paul and Peter's wonderful teaching to the ill-used slaves of their duty. They call upon them to perform all their service, and bear all their sufferings from hard masters, as God's will! And this was done from the heart as unto the Lord! When once all the work of our daily calling is seen to be God's will, and is done heartily for his sake, it need no longer be a hindrance; it will become a great help in enabling us to live wholly to the will of God.

5. Let no secret misapprehension in regard to the doctrine of our entire impotence, and the impossibility of a life truly well pleasing to God, hinder you. Jesus Christ has said: 'My grace is sufficient for you, for all I ask of you, for all you have to do.' Our nature is utterly corrupt and impotent; in our flesh dwelleth no good thing. Living to God's will is only possible, is truly possible, by the power of Jesus Christ resting on us and working in us through the Holy Spirit. Do get firm hold of the truth tha God's Spirit dwells in you as the power for you to do God's will. The grace of the Spirit is only known as you act it out, that is, as in faith you try and do what appears too great to your weakness. Only believe, is the law too for living to the will of God.

6. To live to God's will you need to wait daily for the divine guidance of the Holy Spirit to make that will known to you. Many pray for divine strength to do God's will, but do not think of a divine light first to know God's will. God's will as taught by men or books has not the power to influence. A supernatural teaching wakens the need, and gives the promise of a supernatural power. The will of God is not a number of laws and rules. It is a living light and power, revealed in fellowship with him. The believer who would truly live to the will of God in all things will deeply feel the need of a divine guidance, leading him day by day in the path and the steps of our Lord Jesus. Oh, let us no longer live to the lusts of men, but to the will of God!

Chapter 29

Doing God's Will the Secret of Abiding

*'If any man love the world, the love of the
Father is not in him. And the world passeth
away, and the lust thereof: but he that doeth
the will of God abideth for ever.'*
1 John 2:15,17

Here we have once again the contrast between the two
great powers that contend for mastery over man. We
saw in Romans 12:2, how the great danger that threatens
the consecrated man, and makes a life in God's will
impossible, comes from the side of worldly conformity.
And, in Galatians 1:4, how the one great aim of God's
will in the death of Christ was to deliver us from this pre-

sent evil world. The irreconcilable hostility of the two
principles is brought out here with equal force. 'If any
man love the world, the love of the Father is not in him.'
Freedom from the love of the world by the love of the
Father, utterly expelling it, is the law of the normal
Christian life. And the exercise and discipline by which
the true position is to be maintained, with the love of the
Father and not the love of the world filling the heart and
life, is the doing the will of God: 'He that doeth the will
of God abideth for ever' – abideth unchangingly in God
and an unchangeable love.

What sacred associations there are connected with
that word 'abiding'! Abiding in Christ and in his love
(John 15); abiding in the Son and in the Father (1 John
2: 24,28); God and Christ, the truth and the anointing
abiding in us (1 John 2:14,27; 3:24). The chief thought is
permanent, steadfast, immovable continuance in the
place and the blessing secured to us in Christ and God.
The great secret of the world as its transitoriness – 'it passeth away with all its glory.' And all who are of it partake
of its vanity and uncertainty. And just as far as the Christian breathes its spirit, and allows its love a place in his
heart, he loses the power of abiding. All failure in abiding, all lack of permanence and perseverance in the
Christian life, can have no other cause than that the
spirit and life of the world are robbing the soul of its real
and only strength. The word and will of God are
unchangeable and eternal: 'he that doeth the will of God
abideth for ever.' As a man does the will of God, and in
doing appropriates it, feeds upon and assimilates it, its
very essence enters into his being, and he becomes partaker of its divine strength and unchangeableness. As
the life of God is, so is his will, without variableness and
shadow of turning. And as the will of God is taken up
into the life of the believer, it too is changed into the likeness of the divine life, and becomes freed from all the
variableness and every shadow of turning which is the
mark of this world. 'The world passeth away ... but he
that doeth the will of God abideth for ever.'

'He that doeth the will of God.' It is by doing God's will that the will of God enters into us, and communicates its own divine unchangeableness. The revelation by the Spirit, the knowledge and the contemplation of the love and adoration of the will of God – all these have their place and value. But it is not until we have really done, and are continually doing, the will of God, that it has really mastered us, conquered every enemy, and transformed us into the perfect likeness to itself. It is the doing of the Father's will becomes our meat, that is, the satisfaction of our soul's hunger, and our nourishment, that God himself becomes the strength of our life. It is only then that man is brought back to his original glory. He was created with a will, that into it he might receive the will of God, that God might work his will in him, and so man, in working that will out again, might become the partner and fellow-worker with God in all his works. Jesus Christ, as man, restored human nature to its ideal destiny, and proved what blessedness and glory it is to do the will of God. And redeemed men receive the spirit of Jesus Christ that they, even as he, might find their life in accepting and living and doing nothing but the will of God. As God's will is the only power that upholds and secures the existence of the universe, so that will, done by the believer, is the one security that he never shall be moved. The whole of redemption, all that it reveals of pardoning and sanctifying and preserving grace, has this as its aim and its crown – that man should find his blessedness and his fellowship with God, his likeness to him, in doing his will. 'He that doeth the will of God abideth for ever.'

Blessed abiding! How often believers have mourned and wondered that there was so little abiding peace and joy in their life – that the abiding in Christ and his love was so fluctuating and uncertain. They knew not how near the answer lay as to the cause: 'He that doeth the will of God abideth for ever.' They never noticed how distinctly our Lord had laid down this as the one condition of abiding in him: 'If ye keep my commandments, ye shall abide in my love, even as I have kept my Father's commandments, and abide in his love.' Could words make it plainer that obedience, doing his will, is the secret of abiding? And that if instead of occupying ourselves with the abiding as the object of direct desire, and faith, and prayer, and effort, we were to give up ourselves wholly to keep the commandments and do the will, the abiding would come of itself, because it would be given us by a secret power from on high. 'He that doeth the will of God abideth for ever', and will always and unceasingly abide.

It is to be feared that in the life of the great majority of believers, the doing of the will of the Father has not that overwhelming prominence which it had in the life and teaching of Christ, as in the purpose of the Father. Any revival that is really to affect the spiritual life and elevate the standard of Christian living, must be a revival of holy living, with the vindication of God's claim that every child of his should give himself to do God's will on earth as it is done in heaven. When once God's claim is fully admitted, and without reservation, unconditionally accepted, light will be given as to the divine guidance that will lead us to it, the divine power which makes it possible, the divine certainty that it shall be done. Everything depends upon the simple and whole-hearted acceptance of the great truth, that to be brought back to do the will of God is the one thing we have been redeemed for, and that doing that will is, on earth as in heaven, with us, as with our Lord Jesus, the one secret of abiding in the love of God.

Chapter 30

Prayer According to God's Will

'And this is the confidence that we have in him, that, if we ask anything according to his will, he heareth us: And if we know that he hear us, whatsoever we ask, we know that we have the petitions that we desired of him.'
1 John 5:14–15

God works out his will through the willing and doing of his people. He works in them, all unconsciously to them, to will and to do. While they study his will in his Word, and take it up into their wills and lives and work it out, he is all the while working it out through them. It is a heart and life filled with the love of God's will that becomes the prepared instrument through which God can do his work.

It is with prayer as with work. As God has taken up

into his eternal purpose the co-operation and the labour of his people, so their prayers too. These have their human origin in our desires as wakened by our need or by God's promises, and are yet God's own working in us. They cannot effect any change in the will of God, for they are God's will realising itself through us, and their first condition is that they must be according to God's will. They may indeed, and do, effect a change to what appears to God's will, in what is his will for a time, or as a preliminary or something higher; their real power consists in their being according to God's will, because God works out his will as much through our prayers as our works.

The question has often caused much difficulty: How can I know that my prayers are according to the will of God? The question lies at the very root of our prayer life, as well as of a life in the will of God. It is not easy to give an exhaustive answer. And yet it may be possible to give suggestions that will enable thoughtful Christians to find the answer that meets their own case. The Holy Spirit, where he is to reveal the will of God, where he is also to help us in prayer, must be our teacher.

Let us, first of all, see that we understand the words, 'according to his will', correctly. Many connect them exclusively with 'anything': the thing asked must be according to his will. But there is something more important than this – not only the thing asked for, but the disposition and character of the asker must be according to God's will. In this last lies the real secret of power in prayer. Two Christians both ask for something according to the will of God. He gives it to one and not to another. And why? Because the asking of the one was different from the other. We must connect the words, 'according to his will', with asking. That will include both that the thing asked and the spirit of asking be in harmony with God's will.

That the latter is of primary importance is evident from our Lord's teaching of his disciples. He continually connected the answer to prayer with their state. They must forgive, they must be merciful, they must be humble, they must be believing, they must ask in his name, they must abide in him in keeping his commandments, and his words abide in them; their life must be according to God's will. If they loved him, and kept his commandments, he would pray the Father for them. Only the man whose life and conduct, whose heart and disposition, is according to God's will, can ask according to his will. So James speaks of the fervent, effectual prayer of the righteous man. And John says, 'whatsoever we ask, we receive of him, because we keep his commandments.' It is the life that prays; the prayer has power according to the life; and a life according to God's will can ask according to God's will.

One great reason of this is that the man who lives according to God's will is able spiritually to discern what he may ask for. A Christian may take some promise of God's Word, say, for the conversion of sinners, and begin and pray for some one in the mere power of human love, and without seeking at all to be led by the Spirit into the faith that enables him to pray successfully. It is simply a matter of human will; I would like the conversion of this friend. God wills that all should be saved; I will ask it. While there is no thought of that abiding in Christ through obedience to which the promise of an answer has been given. It is not asking according to the will of God in the deep consciousness of dependence on the Holy Spirit, in that true obedient abiding in Christ Jesus, which alone is truly asking in his name. Doing is the only way to knowing the will of God, and therefore the only way of asking according to his will. As long as I only desire to know God's will with regard to certain things I desire or need, I may find it difficult to know it. A life yielded to and moulded by the will of God will know what and how to pray. A heart seeking to be 'filled with the knowledge of his will in all wisdom and spiritual understanding', and striving fervently to 'stand perfect and complete in all the will of God', will be able joyfully to appropriate the promise, 'This is the confidence that we have in him, that, if we ask anything according to his will, he heareth us.'

Let us try and learn the lessons. Boldness in prayer comes from the assurance that the spirit of asking and the thing we ask are according to the will of God. In all our prayers that we have learnt from his Word, let us take time to realise that they are indeed according to God's loving, mighty will, and therefore sure to be heard. Let us remember how essentially one our lives and our prayers are, and live wholly to God's will – that will ensure our praying according to his will. Let us pray first and wait for the things that God has clearly revealed to be his will, things that concern his love and kingdom and glory – that will give us liberty with the lesser things that concern our interests. Only the Holy Spirit in the spirit of prayer can lead us into the will of God – as we wait on him even in the things we know to be according to God's will, he can give us divine assurance in regard to things that no human reason could believe beforehand to be God's will. Let our first desire in regard to every petition ever be: Lord, teach me how to pray only according to thy will.

God's will is at first a deep, hidden mystery. He that lives to that will as far as he knows it, may count upon being led deeper into it as the manifestation of a holy, mighty, infinite goodness. Let me give myself to it as to infinite love. God works out his will equally by the works and the prayers of his people. Yield yourself equally without reserve to that will in working as in praying, in praying as in working. The absolute joyful surrender of our life to that will, in full obedience and in perfect truth, gives boldness in doing and in asking. And this text, instead of being a stumbling-block, will give us new joy and confidence in prayer, because the prayer according to the will of God must prevail.

Chapter 31

The Glory of God's Will

'They cast their crowns before the throne, singing, "Worthy art thou, our Lord and God, to receive glory and honour and power, for thou didst create all things, and by thy will they existed and were created."'
Revelation 4:10–11

In chapter four of the book of Revelation we have the glory of God as Creator. The living creatures that we in the midst of the throne, and round about the throne, have no rest, day nor night, as they sing, 'Holy, holy, holy, is the Lord God Almighty, which was and is and is to come.' As they show forth the glory of the divine person as him who liveth for ever and ever, the four and twenty elders fall down and worship him in his works, and, casting their crowns before the throne, cry out,

'Worthy art thou, our Lord and our God, to receive glory and honour and power, for thou didst create all things, and by thy will they existed and were created.' Then follows in chapter five the glory of God as Redeemer, where the song of the ransomed, 'Worthy art Thou', and of the angel hosts, 'Worthy is the Lamb', is followed by the adoration of all creatures, 'Blessing, and honour, and glory, and power, be unto him that sitteth upon the throne, and unto the Lamb for ever and ever.' Midway between the worship of God in the glory of his divine being as the holy and everliving one, and his glory of redemption with the Lamb in the midst of the throne, comes the glory of his divine will as the Creator of all. 'Worthy art thou to receive glory, for thou didst create all things, and, by thy will they were created.' Our study of the will of God would be incomplete if we did not learn the place its worship has in heaven, and from that, the place its worship ought to have in our hearts.

In heaven, where all veils are taken away, where everything is seen in the light of God, and God is known, the elders, at the thought that God has been pleased to will creation into existence, fall down on their faces in worship, cast their crowns before the throne, and give him glory because of his will. God's glory shines out in his works. The connecting link between the glory of his divine person and of the works he has made is his will. This is the highest glory of creation, that the God of all glory has willed it, that it is the expression and embodiment of his all-perfect and almighty will, and so bears on it the stamp of his divine glory. The glory of the Creator and the glory of the creature unite in the glory of the divine will, the connecting link between the two. In heaven, creation is seen to be nothing but in every detail the manifestation of the presence, and power, and goodness of God. And the heavenly beings, as the mouthpiece and interpreter of creation, cease not to give glory to this all-creating will. And it is because they see the glory of God's will, and adore it, that they delight in doing it as it is done in heaven.

If we are to do God's will on earth as it is done in heaven, we need the same spirit of adoration and worship. Each of us needs to have our hearts opened to the inconveivably wondrous thought, 'Because of God's will I have, and am what I am. God has willed me into existence. That will maintains me every moment. In virtue of that will I am his redeemed child. On that will I can count to carry out its purpose and effect its object in me. Here I am, the workmanship of the glorious will of the holy and everliving God, as his handiwork partaking of and manifesting his glory. Every moment of my existence, every power of my being, may be the embodiment, the manifestation of God's will. Surely if our eyes and hearts are opened to see this, we too would fall prostrate and worship, saying, 'Thou art worthy to receive the glory, for because of thy will we were created, and are what we are.' And if we have as yet no crowns to cast before the throne, each of us has that which is as the crown of his being – his will, his heart, his life, his love, to offer to him who sits upon the throne, as we say again, 'Thou art worthy to receive the glory, whose will has made us the objects of thy creating and redeeming love.'

It is to show forth in us the glory of his will that God created us. Does not this thought at the close of our meditations give new urgency to the call to live to the will of God? You remember how in our opening chapter we saw what the four great aspects are under which God's will is revealed to us. In regard to each of these, this adoring acknowledgement that we owe our being to God's will, will enable us all the better to give that will the place and the honour to which it has a claim. There is God's will in providence. As I worship the will that brought me forth, and never for a moment ceases its work in me, and connect every trial that in providence it allows to come to me, I shall be enabled to rejoice even in tribulation, and to bear all as part of that blessed will whose I am, and whom I serve. There is God's will in his precepts. As I see how these have their origin in the will of creating love, and are the guides to that co-operation with him which will ensure his perfecting his work in me, my whole heart welcomes every command with the same prostrate worship as that with which it gives glory to him who sits on the throne. There is God's will in his promises. These, too, acquire new preciousness, and certainty, and power, as so many assurances to an intelligent faith that the will that created and upholds all, cares in the minutest detail for our feebleness and need, and provides sufficient grace for a perfect correspondence on our part to what it is working in us. And then there is God's will in his eternal world-wide purpose. The vision of the will that embraces all creation has made me part of it, has made his own glory dependent on its and my own destiny, enlarges my heart to feel that my true and only glory is to yield myself a willing instrument to its service, and to live only that that will may triumph throughout the whole earth.

Oh, the glory of the will of God! In him who sits upon the throne! In the universe which he created to show forth that will! In the heavenly hosts who worship before the throne, where that will is enthroned in glory! In the beloved Son, who came as man to do that will upon earth! In the heart of the believer, who has yielded his life to be conformed to it! In the church, through which that will is working out its eternal purpose in the world! Oh, the glory of the will of God! Let us gaze, and worship, and give glory to God, until the will of God, rule on the throne of our heart as on the throne of heaven, and be done in our life on earth as it is done in heaven.

Lord Jesus, who taught us to pray, 'Thy will be done as in heaven, so on earth', we look to thee, Oh, teach us live thus!

Well Pleasing

Chapter 1

The Secret of Boldness Towards God

'Beloved, if our heart condemn us not, we have boldness toward God; And whatsoever we ask, we receive of him, because we keep his commandments, and do the things that are pleasing in his sight.' 1 John 3:21–22

What a wonderful glimpse into the inner life of John and his fellow-saints! They were not afraid to say to each other: 'We keep his commandments.' They had the consciousness, and dared to rest upon it: We do the things that are pleasing in his sight. They felt that if it were not so, their heart would condemn them. Their boldness toward God would be lost, and all their power in prayer depart. They had learnt one of the most blessed lessons of the Christian life, that to know that we are doing what is pleasing in his sight is one of its highest aims, its deepest joys, the secret of its greatest power.

How many of God's children there are to whom this is a portion of their heritage to which they as yet are entire strangers. They do not believe it possible to live well-pleasing in God's sight. If it were possible they think it most undesirable that one should know it. If one did know it, it would be untrue and unsafe to say it: it could only foster presumption and pride.

How different from the childlike simplicity that cannot think of a child's intercourse with his father without regarding the doing of what is pleasing in his sight as the natural outcome of a father's love and training, and the father's smile as indispensable to its happiness. How different from the simple faith which has really believed that when God makes us his children in Christ, and endows us with the Spirit of his Son, he gives us the capacity to do what pleasess him. He does not expect of us what we cannot do, because he asks nothing for which he does not in the Holy Spirit give us sufficient grace.

We do the things that are pleasing in his sight! How precious the lessons are the words suggest. It is possible to live and act so as to please God. It is possible to know it too – the Father has provided in the Spirit the divine witness that it is so. The possession of this assurance is the secret of liberty and power with God and man. Of a life in the fullness of the joy and strength of God this is an essential element. Such a life is the simple duty and privilege of every child of God.

There are many who acknowledge all this, and lament that the absence of this consciousness is a continual cloud in their sky. With deep longing of heart they ask what is needed to live such a life. God's Word alone can give the answer: God's Spirit alone can teach us to find the answer in the Word. But to those who are willing, in true simplicity, to yield to that Word, and to the teaching of the Spirit, the secret will be shown.

Let us go through the Word and listen to what it has to say to us on this wonderful life of pleasing God. It will be a great step if we can get our hearts thoroughly settled in the truth. Such a life has been, it is the life God wants us to live, it is an essential element in a holy, healthy Christian life. This will lead us on to see how it is only in Christ Jesus, in living and abiding union with him, that we can be pleasing. But also, how it is a sure and blessed starting point. Through Jesus as the door I enter into the Father's love and am most pleasing to him. I shall then feel the need of the precious truth that Jesus is able to keep me in the Father's love all the day, and, through the Holy Spirit in me, so to strengthen and sanctify, that all I do shall be pleasing in his sight. I shall see that it is the work of the holy triune God – God himself by his Holy Spirit working in me that which is pleasing in his sight through Jesus Christ. I shall then understand how, instead of lifting up, just this consciousness will deeply humble: God's working will be so clear that there will be no thought but that of my being within. And just as the light manifests and bears witness to itself, so the Holy Spirit will by his very witness that what I do is pleasing give the witness too that it is God who hath wrought it all.

'We do the things that are pleasing in his sight.' Oh! the blessed childlike joy of living thus, in the full sunshine of the Father's love! Oh! the blessed boldness toward God it gives, and the power in prayer it brings! By your grace, my Father, let this be my life.

Chapter 2

God Himself Works It in You

> *'Now the God of peace ... Make you perfect*
> *in every good work to do his will, working in*
> *you that which is well-pleasing in his sight.'*
> Hebrews 13:20–21

It is no wonder Christians hesitate to believe in the possibility of living well-pleasing to God in all things, as long as they think that it is something they have to accomplish. But how all becomes changed, and all doubts vanish, when they fully believe what our text says – that it is God himself who works it in them. If he undertakes to do it, it can be: if he offers to do it, it becomes a duty to accept the offer; it becomes a sin not to do what is pleasing in his sight.

Note the ground on which this work of God in us rests. He is 'the God of peace, who brought again from that dead the great shepherd of the sheep with the blood of the everlasting covenant.' In that he perfected the work of our redemption, gave us the proof of his power to overcome sin, and the pledge of what he would do for us. And now, just as surely as God wrought within the darkness and hopelessness of the grave of Christ his secret mighty work and raised him up, will he work in the apparently hopeless sinfulness of your heart the same mighty work: it is a resurrection power. He engages to work in you that which is pleasing in his sight.

'In you.' There is a work that God has done for us in the past to which we are invited to look as an assurance of what he seeks to do in us in the present. Yes, the work in us is nothing but the continuation of the work for us. The same power is being exerted: the same blessed result is sure, with this difference: He wrought the work in us, now we are alive. He waits for our consent, for our co-operation, for our faith. He asks that we shall yield ourselves to him into the death, that we shall yield, as Christ did, when he said, 'Into thy hands I commend my spirit.' He will raise up the divine life in us in the same power, in which he raised Christ.

'Working in you that which is well-pleasing in his sight.' Let us try and realise the wonderful working of God. We see it in nature. How does God clothe the grass or the lily with its beauty, the vine or the apple tree with its fruitfulness? Not from without. He works within. He gives and supports an inner life out of which the outer form grows and flourishes. Even so, or rather, much more so, in his redeemed child. The new life he gives us in Christ's resurrection can only live and thrive as it is in actual connection each moment with the same source from which it came. The living God must each moment maintain it. The immediate and unceasing operation of his Holy Spirit is the essential condition of a holy life. The direct, intentional and continual exercise of God's energy is needed for every moment that our life is to be what he wants it to be, that we are to do what is pleasing in his sight. God must do it, or it will not be done. God can do it, and therefore it can be done. God will do it, if we allow him.

'Working in you that which is well-pleasing in his sight.' Not at times, not fitfully or feebly, but always and effectually. Shall we not take courage, and begin to look upon the call to walk worthy of the Lord unto all well-pleasing as what God in all earnest expects of us? It is not only our position in Christ that is to make us well-pleasing. By no means, that is the beginning, the planting of the tree. But the fruit is to be pleasing – the things we do, our daily disposition and thoughts and actions are to be pleasing in his sight. Let us begin to take it in earnest as God's will concerning us, as much as that we should not lie or steal.

And let no one fear lest the height of the demand make us hopeless. Its very height is our hope. As we see how entirely it is beyond our own strength, it will draw us with a mighty attraction to the promise: 'The God of peace make you perfect to do his will, working in you that which is well-pleasing in his sight.' The God who wrought the mighty resurrection miracle in Christ is working in you in that very same power and with the very same object. His work in Christ and in you is all one. Do believe this. And begin to be still in his holy presence, and to count upon his divine, direct, continuous inworking, and then to do the one thing he asks, that you first yield yourself and every faculty for him to work in you both to will and to do according to his good pleasure. He will do it: He will work in you 'that which is well-pleasing in his sight.'

Chapter 3

The Mark of
God's Child

*'Children, obey your parents in all things: for
this is well-pleasing in the Lord.'*
Colossians 3:20

One of the strongest and purest motives by which we
seek to influence a child is that of giving pleasure to
parents or teachers. The more tender and truly childlike
the young heart is, the quicker it is to catch every indication, given in the face of one it loves and looks up to, of
pleasure or of grief. The mark of indifference it cannot
bear: it feels it has a right to be noticed and its love or service rewarded with an approving smile.

In writing to the children, to remind them that the first
duty of child-like and child-religion is obedience to
parents, Paul appeals to the child-heart with this the
highest motive, 'for this is well-pleasing in the Lord.' He

would have the children know that every act of obedience to parents is pleasing to Jesus. He would have them
remember this as a stimulus and a motive: he would have
them count it a reward and a joy. The happiness of the
earthly home was to be brightened to the obedient child
by a sense of having pleased the Lord in heaven.

To give pleasure, and to receive the assurance of having pleased, is indeed one of the strongest motives, and
one of the deepest joys in the life of a child. And it is only
the child of God who is to be shut out from this source of
strength and happinesss? The relation of a child to a
parent is, in every possible aspect, of duty, of love, of
trust, of chastisement, of dependence, taken as the
illustration of our relation to the heavenly Father. And
it is to be only in this one respect, in the very deepest joy
the child-like gives, that the child of God may not hope
to have reproduced in his own life, what makes the child-
life so beautiful and so blessed? No, indeed. The father
does want his child to live in his smile; the father has provided grace and strength to enable him to do it; the
father does want his child to know that he is pleasing,
and will by his Holy Spirit give the blessed witness that is
so in very truth.

There is a religion, clinging most firmly, as it thinks, to
Scripture and evangelical truth, from which this sunshine of the Christian life is almost entirely banished.
The soul walks in the light of pardon and acceptance.
But it is a clouded sky, not the bright sunshine. To cultivate a sense of our own unworthiness and abiding sinfulness is with such counted the only safeguard against
superficiality and pride. They do not understand that
just he may have the deepest conviction of utter corruption and impotence, who, in total despair of soul as
utterly loathsome and hopelessly evil, has given it into
the death of Jesus, now to let him live and work within.
Nor do they see how this is the true meaning of being
well-pleasing in Christ Jesus, having him to live and
work that we ever present ourselves before the Father in
Christ as the one in whom all our works are wrought.

Child of God, let me urge you not to rest content in your communion with the Father without the enjoyment of this wonderful privilege. There is not a family life so happy as that of the father with his children: the joy of pleasing him is one of the deepest elements. A child cannot know whether he pleases his father, when that father is a hard man, impatient of every failure, inconsiderate of a child's weakness, taking no account of its loving work and effort. But a loving father – a child can know whether he has tried to please, whether he has succeeded, and whether the father has given the smile of approval. Let the intention to please God in everything as the best and happiest thing in the world, become the inspiration of every day's work. Do not hesitate to offer every prayer, every performance of duty, every act of love and kindness, to the Father as done for him, and seek the assurance of his approval. Gradually but surely, the sense of walking in his light and in his smile will grow stronger and clearer. This will bow the soul into a deeper humility than ever the sense of its sins could work. The pursuit of this will make the absolute need of God's working in us, and Christ's dwelling in us, and the Spirit's leading us, more deeply felt, and will urge us to claim them as indispensable to the life of a child of God. And the pleasure and delight and love with which the Father looks upon the Son will be on us and in us, because the Spirit of the Son is seen in this too – the confiding trust with which we live our life as offered to the Father, and makes his pleasure our chiefest joy.

Chapter 4

Its Secret

'*I do nothing of myself, but as the Father taught me ... And he that sent me is with me; he hath not left me alone; for I do always the things that are pleasing to him.*' John 8:28–29

'I do nothing of myself: I do always the things that are pleasing in his sight.' Here is the secret of a life in all things well-pleasing: doing nothing of myself. Where self is nothing, everything is pleasing to the Father.

'I do nothing of myself, but as the Father taught me.' – It is the spirit of entire self-abnegation, the ceasing from our own wisdom and our own strength, the spirit of teachableness and dependence upon God – it is this spirit of the meek and lowly lamb of God that fits for always doing the things that are pleasing in his sight.

'I do nothing of myself ... And he that sent me is with me; he hath not left me alone.' God never leaves those whom he sends. As needful as it is that he sends, no less needful that he should abide with those he sends, and not leave them. Just as the tree every moment through a hundred years lives only by that life which began in the seed and unceasingly works upwards as its strength and growth, so every moment the sent one needs the very same immediate working of God's power that sent him out. As distinct and direct as the work of God in giving life or sending forth, is the power that must inspire each work that is done. The continual, immediate indwelling and operation of God is the only secret of works pleasing to him, because it is the only secret of deliverance from self, by the expulsive power of a mightier presence. I do nothing of myself: and he that sent me is with me. He hath not left me alone.

'He hath not left me alone; for I do always the things that are pleasing to him.' The abiding presence of God, a presence which is in the power of a ceaseless indwelling and inworking, is both cause and effect of the doing of things pleasing in his sight. It is the cause: the beginning is all with him: he sends, and works, and does not leave. It is the effect too: the doing the things pleasing in his sight proves and increases the capacity for his fuller presence, and opens the way for the divine complacency to enter us and possess the very inmost life.

Such was the life of Jesus. And such our life can be, because he came to be our life, and lives in heaven 'to fill all things', to live his life in his members. The example he gave, and the teaching in which he unfolded the meaning of that example, are to show us our calling, to waken our desire, and to guide our faith. As God was in Christ, so Christ is in us. All his work for us, all that he outwardly accomplished and manifested, has but one aim – that we should live in him and he in us. The same Christ who dwelt on earth with us, now dwells on earth in us. And every new discovery of what he was on earth, is a discovery of what he is now as our life within us. Christ always doing the things that are pleasing in the Father's sight – this is the Christ who dwells in us.

Let us seek to know him in his hidden indwelling in the

Spirit, from what he was when in the body. I do nothing of myself: there is the beginning of all. Self nothing: God all – this was Christ's theology. By this rule he lived, in this spirit he died. He gave up himself into the helplessness of death, trusting God to raise him and give a new life, more glorious than he had before. It is in fellowship with the death of Christ that we are dead to self and learn to say: I do nothing of myself.

With the death the life of Christ becomes ours. Christ the living one rises in our hearts as the light of God, and we can say with him: I do nothing of myself, but as the Father taught me. And he that sent me, is with me; He hath not left me alone; for I do always the things that are pleasing in his sight.

O that all who speak of 'Jesus only', 'Christ is all', might see that this is the Jesus who dwells in the heart. One who always does the things that are pleasing in his sight. This is what he offers us as his work in us. Let this be the Christ we believe in, the Christ to whom we offer our heart, in whose name we draw near to God. His life shall be ours, and ours like his: I do nothing of myself: I always do the things that are pleasing in his sight.

Chapter 5

This Is the Lord's Doing

'He hath done whatsoever he pleased.'
Psalm 115:3

'Whatsoever the Lord pleased, that hath he done.' Psalm 135:6

These words we ordinarily understand of the power of God. Whatsoever he wills, he is able to do. But they also suggest another truth, that all that is pleasing to God is done by himself. He doeth whatsoever pleaseth him.

In our study of what is well-pleasing to God, and of how we can live the life of well-pleasing, this thought is of the utmost importance. What is the reason that we think that what we have done never can be pleasing to God? It is because we think of it as being done by ourselves. We are so conscious – would God we were more so – of the corruption of our nature as children of Adam, of the utter unholiness of self and all that comes from it, that we count it impossible for anything we do to be pleasing to God. We lose out of sight the most important element: that God himself is working in us. Amidst all that an earnest, upright heart discovers of sin and imperfection, there is a power of divine life working underneath the surface. It is God who is working there. Amid our imperfect efforts God knows and notices his own works. Their divine eternal worth is to him infinitely more than their human temporary imperfection. And in them, and in the man who is doing them, however imperfectly. God takes pleasure. And God would have us know it: He doeth whatsoever is pleasing to him.

A due appreciation of this truth would bring us blessing in more than one way. It would bring us out into a large place, and brighten our daily life with the actual sense of the father's smile resting on us. It would awaken within us a previously unknown tenderness of desire to do nothing but what is indeed pleasing to him. Grieving him, instead of being looked upon, as it now so often is, as a fatal necessity from which there is no deliverance, would become an intolerable thought. Our faith would be strengthened, that he who takes pleasure in us amid all our weakness, will in very deed fulfil the good pleasure of his goodness, himself working in us that which is pleasing in his sight. And so, best of all, we should learn what it is to yield ourselves to the faith of the power that worketh in us, we should cherish the consciousness that the Holy Spirit is indeed in us, working in us both to will and to do.

Yes, God is indeed all in all. There are diverse operations, but it is 'the same God who worketh all in all.' There can be nothing that is pleasing to God but what is wrought by himself. There is nothing that is wrought by himself but is infinitely pleasing to him. There is nothing therefore in which he asks us to please him, in which we may not count that he will do it himself. And because he asks that our whole life, all we think, and all we do, shall be pleasing in his sight, we must believe that he expects nothing of us but what he himself is willing to work.

Let me ask each reader to pause a moment now for the personal application, and mark well the lessons that this truth brings us. I can of myself do nothing that is well-pleasing to God. God calls me to walk worthy of him unto all well-pleasing. God promises to work in me that which is pleasing in his sight. Whatsoever pleased the Lord that hath he done. On my part nothing is needed but the determined desire and purpose to please him in all things, through his own power working it in me. And he works it in me in no other way than through that Spirit of his Son, who dwells in me. This is the one thing I need: to recognise, to wait upon, to yield to that blessed Spirit, who, as a hidden seed of all divine life and strength, is even now in me. A life pleasing to God is a promise and possibility: the Holy Spirit is the earnest of our inheritance, the pledge that I shall inherit these promises. Let me turn inward, and with that new heart, which God has given within me, all cleansed by the blood, all permeated and possessed by the Spirit, let me yield myself to God working all that pleases him. And let a life in the pleasure of God, in doing his pleasure, and enjoying the sense of his pleasure, henceforth be my hope and my delight.

Chapter 6

The Lord Taketh Pleasure in His People

'Let them sing praises unto him ... For the Lord taketh pleasure in his people: he will beautify the meek with salvation.'
Psalm 149:3–4

What pleasure an owner takes in his property; a merchant in his business; an artist in his work; a teacher in his pupils; a father in his children. Everywhere pleasure in what we own or are occupied with is the motive and the joy and the reward of self-sacrifice. The joy and the health and the strength of love is the pleasure it finds in its object.

And shall there in him, of whom all earthly relationships are the feeble shadow, shall there in him be no pleasure in the work of his hand? No, it is indeed true: The Lord taketh pleasure in his people.

When that was said of Israel, they were indeed very far from being what they ought to be. And still God took pleasure in them. Just as grace looked not to merit, in choosing and saving and blessing that people, God looks as little at merit as the measure of his pleasure. He sees his own work being carried in them, in the midst of all imperfection and unfaithfulness. He sees the work of his own Spirit in all the integrity of purpose and earnestness of effort with which his people seek him, and they are to him a source of infinite pleasure. Each heavenward striving, each sacrifice for his name, each act of prayer and of praise, is valued by him with a value above what we can conceive. And where we count ourselves very discerning in seeing sin and failure and mingled motive, God rejoices with a father's delight over the true, the divine, the eternal that he sees working through it all. The Lord takes pleasure in his people. He sees reason for it; and it is to him the joy and the rejoicing of his heart.

The Psalmist has lifted up his soul, and looked into the very heart of God. He would have us look there too. Alas, how many children of God there are who have never done so. They have allowed themselves to believe that God has taken no pleasure in them or their life. They believe in his love, and pity, and compassion, covering and forgetting their sins; but that, day by day, or hour by hour, he takes pleasure in them – they count the very thought of such a thing to be dangerous, a piece of presumption and pride.

Believer, listen to the message the Old Testament gives you: The Lord takes pleasure in his people. Do believe that, at this very moment, if you will be still and look up, you may say: Yes Father, you are even now taking pleasure in me. You see these wishes that rise, these longings after yourself; you see how my only trust is in Jesus, and how it is indeed my only desire to serve you with my whole heart; I believe you take plesure in them and in me. The consciousness of failure, the fear of unfaithfulness, the doubt of my own uprightness: you know how these arise and darken all; but I will believe, yes, I do believe even now: my Lord does take pleasure in me.

It is not the strong and healthy child, but the sickly and the feeble one in which the mother often finds the greatest pleasure. Every token of affection for all her care, every little sign of progress and advancement is often cause of exquisite delight. Child of God, however feeble, do learn with every prayer you offer, and every duty you seek to perform, to couple the upward look, and the trusting faith that says: the Lord takes pleasure in his people. Cultivate the habit practically and perseveringly, and it will grow, and your soul will learn how sweet it is to trust, and praise, to worship and serve a God who takes pleasure in you and all you do in his presence.

'Let them sing praises unto him ... For the Lord taketh pleasure in his people.' Yes, we may depend upon it that as we learn to know our God thus, to count upon his smile, to dwell in his heart and his love, our soul will be stirred to praise as never before. We shall find that we have new reason for it, and new pleasure in it, because we have found that it gives real pleasure to him.

The Africa Evangelical Fellowship

The AEF is an international evangelical mission. For more information about their work, please contact them at their International office, 17 Westcote Road, Reading, Berks RG3 2DL.

The AEF has hundreds of opportunities for both long and short term service in evangelism, church planting, education, medical administration, youth work and other practical fields.

Other AEF offices are:-

Australia
PO Box 292
Castle Hill
New South Wales 2154

Canada
470 McNicoll Avenue
Willowdale
Ontario M2H 2E1

USA
PO Box 2896
Boone
North Carolina 28607

United Kingdom
30 Lingfield Road
Wimbledon
London SW19 4PU

Zimbabwe
99 Gaydon Road
Graystone Park
Borrowdale
Harare

South Africa
Rowland House
6 Montrose Avenue
Claremont 7700

New Zealand
PO Box 1390
Invercargill

Europe
5 Rue de Meautry
94500 Champigny-sur-Marne
France